SELF-DISCIPLINE & MENTAL TOUGHNESS FOR SUCCESS & HAPPINESS (2 IN 1)

DEVELOP YOUR DISCIPLINE, BUILD HEALTHY DAILY HABITS & OVERCOME PROCRASTINATION TO FULFIL YOUR POTENTIAL & FIND TRUE FREEDOM

STEWART HUNTER

DEVON HOUSE
PRESS

CONTENTS

Part I
THE ROAD TO SELF-DISCIPLINE AND
MENTAL TOUGHNESS

1. A Full Dive on What You're Aiming For   3

Part II
WHAT'S GETTING IN YOUR WAY

2. Your #1 Enemy is Yourself   17
3. A World Full of Distractions   47

Part III
UNEARTHING YOUR REASON TO CHANGE

4. Start with the Way You Think   67
5. Engineering a Disciplined Life   80
6. Reaching for Your Highest Goals and Aiming for 94
   True Freedom

Part IV
LEARN TO LOVE THE PROCESS, YOU
CAN'T SKIP IT

7. Developing Discipline   117
8. Strengthening Mental Toughness   131
9. Keep Calm and ...   143
10. Breaking Old Routines and Creating Effective Habits   162
11. Overcoming Procrastination and Making Friends 174
    with Time
12. It's Within Your Grasp, Literally   187

Part V

APPLYING DISCIPLINE AND MENTAL
TOUGHNESS IN YOUR LIFE

13. You Must Unstuck Yourself   199
14. Keeping Yourself Fit and Healthy   209

Conclusion – Things That You Shouldn't Forget   219

I

THE ROAD TO SELF-DISCIPLINE AND MENTAL TOUGHNESS

A FULL DIVE ON WHAT YOU'RE AIMING FOR

W e begin the journey towards better self-discipline and mental toughness by taking a look at what we're looking to do. In this chapter, we're going to dive into what discipline is, and how you should view it.

We'll also discuss whether or not mental toughness is something to rely on for everyday things or in times where the pressure is on and you won't settle for anything less than your best. We'll discuss more about the definition of mental toughness and how its viewed (while comparing it to how it should be viewed).

Every journey is not easy. And you will come across some obstacles as you travel from Point A to Point B. No one is born with discipline and mental toughness.

This book will show you how to build on those things from the ground up. Now, let's talk a bit about discipline.

WHAT DOES IT MEAN TO BE DISCIPLINED?

Discipline is something that is taught. It's not something that we're born with. Discipline means being able to perform a task whether you like to do it or not. If you set up some rules and standards that you want to adhere by, following them will be defined as discipline.

For example, let's say you want to be out of bed by 5AM. You learn to discipline yourself by getting up at that time even if the idea of sleeping in another hour is tempting. Being disciplined means you're behaving in a certain way.

But why is it that people view discipline as some "bad word"? We'll explain that in the next section.

DISCIPLINE SOUNDS LIKE...SO HOW IS IT DIFFERENT?

Most people view discipline as a bad thing. Specifically, the word "discipline" is anchored to the event when someone does something wrong (like stealing cookies from the cookie jar), they need to be disciplined for it. However, the use of the word is in a different context.

You won't be grounded for a month for being lazy or having a poor mindset. The kind of discipline we are aiming for is in the context of restraining yourself. If there is something you need to scale back on or quit entirely (bad habits and such), you'll need to discipline yourself.

You need to restrain yourself from something that may hold power over you. Allowing yourself to give into vices will not only validate the fact that you are giving power to it, but it proves that your level of discipline or restraint is low.

Not giving in is a sure sign of strength. Especially when we're talking about mental strength and toughness. But why is it so hard to do?

The rewards of being disciplined and restraining yourself from making bad decisions is within easy reach. It's like a pot of gold sitting in front of you just waiting to be claimed by you. Yet, somehow, we make it impossible to achieve it.

We tend to get comfortable with our bad habits and vices. And depending on what it is, we pay the price for it thanks to short-term and long-term effects. For example, let's take a look at procrastination.

You have a big project coming up. The deadline is a few weeks out. The sooner you get it done, the better.

But you decide to put it off because you have a comfortable amount of time to "goof off" before the due date. So, you say to yourself "Screw it. It can wait". You do some of your favorite things like play video games, veg out on the couch and watch Netflix, or whatever else.

Before you know it, two weeks pass and suddenly you're under a lot of pressure to finish the project. You allow the pressure to get to you mentally and you feel like you're about to go crazy. You sacrifice sleep, put off other important things, and what have you.

You soon come to the realization that had you got this done sooner, perhaps you wouldn't feel like a zombie for a few days. You put things off that you think you're going to do tomorrow (but never do until the last minute). Now let's compare that to the other way around.

Close your eyes for a moment. Imagine you have already read this book, adopted the principles you've learned to become more disciplined and mentally tough. Now, let's replay that same scenario.

You have a project coming up. It's due a few weeks from now. You think to yourself, perfect maybe I can get it out of the way so I can do what I want in my free time. So, you chip away at the project on day one.

You pace yourself and take your time. You're not in a rush to get it done (and if you did that, the quality would show for it). You spend a few hours per day while ignoring texts, Facebook notifications, and so on.

One of the notifications on your phone unbeknownst to you is some update of your favorite game. You probably don't care at this point because you have more important things to do. Sometimes, procrastinating can work in your favor when it's something that tends to be a distraction (but we digress).

So, a week and a half has passed. The project is done and ahead of schedule. Sure, you decided to stay up a little later because you had so much fun doing something that keeps you busy.

The quality is impressive. Nothing is half-assed. And your boss, client, project partners, or colleagues are quite happy with the amount of effort and detail you put into it.

The work shows that you cared about investing your time wisely in the important things. That gives you a level of unmatchable confidence. And it boosts your mental toughness in the process.

That's because you've learned how to discipline yourself by placing priorities over all else. You've put the interests of others over yourself (not in a pushover sort of way). Someone wanted to get a project done and you managed to put in the time and effort to help them out.

As a result, you are handsomely rewarded for all of your efforts (and get a nice pay bonus as the cherry on top). Will discipline and mental toughness earn you a raise at your job? We can't guarantee that.

But we can say that discipline and mental toughness does have its rewards. When you are able to restrain yourself from making poor decisions, you will feel good about it mentally. Your level of discipline will not only affect you, but it will affect others as well.

For example, if the project you did is in poor quality then it will affect the people you work with. The client will view your company unfavorably and may shift gears and work with someone else. This will tarnish your company's image and it can lead to some tough decisions for your boss both in the short-term and long-term (which may include cutting you loose as part of the cutback process so their company stays afloat).

Discipline, whether you have it or lack it, will trigger a domino effect like nothing else. That is why discipline is so important. If you fail to use it, who knows what kind of effect it will have on you and others in a negative way.

HOW RELIABLE IS MENTAL TOUGHNESS?

Mental toughness is usually a term that we hear in sports. One of the biggest proponents of it is Bill Belichick. And it's one of the core reasons why the New England Patriots had been one of the most successful teams in football history winning a total of six Super Bowl titles.

Belichick said the following: "Mental toughness is continuing to do the right things even when things aren't going right for you personally". Read that last sentence again. Hammer meets nail.

The truth is, discipline and mental toughness go hand in hand. There are some things that have to get done, but you're having a bad day and you'd rather just lay on the couch, relax, and forget about everything. You could be having the worst day ever, but it's incumbent upon you to do your part even if you don't feel like it.

Let's take a look at another example where mental toughness and discipline go together. Suppose you are just reading through a comment thread on social media. And someone decided to get nasty with someone based on some difference in opinion.

You read the comment and the temptation to fire back an angry and equally nasty reply appears. Mind you, the comment wasn't directly towards you. You have the choice to just ignore it and move on (even if it goes against what you feel you should do personally) or get sucked right in and prove yourself that like the dimwit who left the nasty comment, you are as undisciplined and not as mentally tough.

The truth is anyone who tries to engage in these comment wars by putting down someone is lacking in discipline and mental toughness. What bothered them to get to that point? It's true what they say: don't stoop down to their level (in this case, their level of mental toughness and discipline...which is lacking).

Is mental toughness reliable? The answer is yes. It's only unreliable if you choose not to use it.

Mental toughness is built so you can consistently perform at a level where you can get the job done and never compromise on quality. Mental toughness allows you to fine tune yourself and get better. And it protects your level of success now and in the future.

You don't have to always rely on talent. You rely on your consistency, your willingness to work hard, and let nothing get in the way of your goals (whether they are short-term or long-term goals). Mental toughness is an element that is needed in leadership.

Like discipline, mental toughness will affect others in a positive way. Specifically, mentally tough leaders will have the backs of those who follow them. They will build them up and encourage them to do better (as opposed to talk them down).

When a leader gets the team going, they work together as one mentally tough unit and achieve that one common goal they want.

Case in point, Bill Belichick's leadership (and his "Patriot Way" of discipline) led to the number of Super Bowl titles and cementing himself into one of football's greatest coaches.

MENTAL TOUGHNESS SOUNDS LIKE…SO HOW IS IT DIFFERENT?

When people think of mental toughness, they think it sounds like this: Be tough, show no emotion, and keep doing what you do. In other words, don't let anyone see you cry or get angry. Just get on with it like some emotionless robot.

Thais couldn't be farther from the truth. You shouldn't withhold emotions. If you are going through a rough day, it's okay to use that emotion to get through the pain.

It's okay to cry when you've had a rough day. And it doesn't matter if anyone sees it or not. And it's okay to voice your frustrations and anger.

As long as you keep yourself in check and never let it get out of control, invoking negative emotions to get through the pain will help you become mentally tougher. You can make a more positive impression if you know how to maintain a positive attitude while managing your emotions at a healthy level (compared to being an emotionless robot, which makes you look bland and boring).

What mental toughness should actually sound like is having a positive mindset. You're accepting of the fact that failure will happen multiple times. When it does, you should move forward with a sense of knowing that things will go well in the future.

Failure is not an indication that it's the end of the world. Nor is it an indicator that you should give up and resign to a life of mediocrity or whatever else. Also, managing your own stress in stressful situations is also a defining pillar in mental toughness.

Regardless if things are going wrong or when the pressure is on, the last thing you want to do is fold and give up. Even when working through the stress, there will always be a reward at the end of the tunnel. And that sense of accomplishment will give you the dopamine rush you deserve.

Mental toughness is built on the following four pillars: Challenge, Control, Commitment, and Confidence. When things get challenging, you'll want to be in control with as much of it as possible. See it through to the end and you'll have the confidence in conquering every single challenge you face.

Control is the most important of the four. Either you control the stress and pressure, or it controls you. You have the power to rise above any challenge, so don't let it be the other way around.

LIKE EVERY OTHER ROAD IN OUR LIFE, IT'S BOUND TO GET BUMPY

It's true what they say: there are roads in life that will get bumpy. Some of them will have obstacles that will be challenging to navigate. But that's all part of the journey.

It's a road less traveled. But unbeknownst to most is that you get to your destination faster. Before you say anything else, this road is no shortcut.

Compare that to another road. It's smooth, flat, and has plenty of light. You see it as far as the horizon.

Does it go to the same destination? Yes, it does. Nothing in the way, no roadblocks, no obstacles.

Seems simple enough to travel on it, right? What could possibly go wrong? You travel down the road and get to the end when suddenly you find yourself falling a thousand feet below.

It's irrefutable proof that what can go wrong, will go wrong. Things can go "smoothly" and suddenly you drop off and lose control. You survive the fall miraculously. But the journey gets a lot tougher (not to mention it takes a longer period of time to get to your destination).

Simply put, you can choose to accept the fact that there will be challenges and bumpy roads along the way. Or you can take the "easy" route and suddenly see yourself falling off a "Cliff" when you least expect it.

Now that you are aware of this, the question you'll be asking yourself on a regular basis is "where do I go from here"? If you see yourself stuck on this bumpy road and you have a hard time navigating the obstacles, you can always ask for help.

It's easy for us to be stubborn and eschew the idea for fear of embarrassment. But no one has ever died from asking someone for help on how to get from one point to the next in their journey towards self-discipline and mental toughness. Seek out the people who you believe are the most disciplined and mentally toughest people you know and ask questions.

At that point, you can learn from them about their own journey that helped them build their self-discipline and mental toughness. They've been there and done that. They know the roads are full of bumps and potholes.

Do you have to copy everything down to the letter of what they need? Not really. But you can find some excellent nuggets of advice and ideas to help you better navigate the obstacles while traveling the rough roads towards self-discipline and mental toughness.

RECAP

At this point, you already know the real truth about discipline and mental toughness. We've already debunked the age-old myths that discipline is a bad thing. And that mental toughness doesn't mean being an emotionless robot either.

Discipline is where restraint comes into play when something that holds enough power to suck you in to do the opposite of what you want. It's easy for us to get that extra half hour of sleep. Or to rest on our laurels for hours on end and binge watch our favorite shows on Netflix.

Your lack of discipline is something that not only will affect you, but it will affect other people as well. It's a domino effect like nothing else.

Discipline and mental toughness indeed go hand in hand (especially when control is one of the key blocks to the latter).

In order to establish discipline and mental toughness, it's all about having control. Either you control yourself or let the vices of procrastination and bad habits control you. On top of that, you'll need to be aware that challenges will exist.

It will be up to you to conquer those challenges while managing your stress at the same time. You'll see it through to the end no matter how many obstacles you face. When you conquer the challenges, you increase your confidence.

The more confidence you have, beating the challenges will be as easy and effortless as ordering your favorite pizza. Now that you have a full dive on what we're aiming for, it's time to identify the obstacles that stand in the way.

In the next chapter, we'll be covering several common roadblocks and obstacles that you may have encountered (and will likely do so again) when you're on the journey towards discipline and mental toughness. Strap in, turn the page, and let's go for a ride.

II

WHAT'S GETTING IN YOUR WAY

2

YOUR #1 ENEMY IS YOURSELF

Pow! Right away, we kick off this chapter with a knock into reality. Like the name of the chapter, the number one enemy, your archnemesis in achieving self-discipline and mental toughness is none other than yourself. There really is no point in blaming anyone else or situation for this.

It's easy to blame someone for things. Especially when it comes to a lack of discipline and mental weakness. In fact, it's a major symptom of both.

In this chapter, we're going to talk about what makes you public enemy number one when it comes to this ultimate goal we are trying to achieve. We've also got one more little surprise to spring on you (and to warn you, it's kind of an unwelcome one). Once you find out what it is, we'll discuss what you can do about it so you can be on the path to positive instead of walking around in negative circles.

Now that you know that you are your own worst enemy in terms of trying to be more disciplined and mentally tough, let's get to the common issues that make that happen (even if you don't know about them already):

YOUR PRIORITIES ARE ALL OVER THE PLACE AND YOU CAN'T FOCUS ON ONE THING

Of course, this is common for almost everyone. We tend to work on one thing then shift to the next thing ten seconds later and repeat the process. It's a vicious never-ending cycle.

It's easy for us to lose attention with one task because we're now paying attention to one other thing. But that amount of attention that task is getting is short-lived and fleeting because we see yet another thing to pay attention to. Before we know it, we lose track of it all and it's nothing more than a huge confusing mess.

The key word here is prioritization. It's about putting the most critical task first among others before the other. So why is it so hard to do?

That's because we mix our priorities with our personal goals. Sure, those goals are important. But there are things that have to be done beforehand.

You'll want to plan out your clear priorities before the day begins. And there are a few reasons why that is:

- With clear, planned out priorities you can be able to structure your day. You get the most critical task done before moving onto the next one. Some things have to be done and the window is tight in terms of deadlines. The closer the deadline, the more critical it is.

- It will show you how to effectively use the words "yes" and "no". Regarding the latter, you're going to learn how to say it without breaking a sweat or stressing about it. You'll need to learn how to say "no" to things that are not as urgent nor important. We'll explain this further in the chapter.

- You'll be investing your time wisely and sort of by force (depending on how critical the task is). With a set plan with your priorities ahead of the pack, you'll know exactly where to spend your time and how long. Not to mention, you will be prepared to get the task done without sacrificing any quality. Keep in mind that there is little to no room for half-assing it.

- You'll learn how to focus on ONE task at a time. Sure, people will say that they are good at multitasking. Just because they say it doesn't mean you have to do it either. In fact, resist the urge to attempt multi-tasking as much as possible. You're only human and you can only do as much as possible. Instead of multitasking, delegate if necessary.

One of the best ways to plan and prioritize your tasks is to take a page out of Dwight D. Eisenhower, a military leader who later became President of the United States. Eisenhower devised a way to put his most critical tasks ahead of everything else.

This became known as the Eisenhower Matrix. To get a sense of what this looks like, pay attention to the following chart:

Urgent/Important	Do or don't do?
Urgent AND Important	Do
Urgent BUT Not Important	Delegate (but do if time allows it)
Not urgent BUT Important	Do it, but at a later time
Not urgent AND Not Important	Don't do it

The Eisenhower Matrix is separated into four quadrants determined on urgency and importance. If the task is urgent and important, that is your most critical task. And it must be done before all else.

If the task is urgent but not important, you will likely opt to delegate to someone who can get it done for you (assuming the level of urgency is high). If you are lucky enough to have a small enough time window to get it done, go for it. But use your better judgement in such a situation.

Next is not urgent but important. Indeed, these tasks are important enough for you to pay attention to. However, the timing of getting them down is not as urgent. You could schedule to get it done the following day or the day after.

Lastly, we have the not urgent and not important things. This is where a lot of people are. They do the tasks that cause us to procrastinate and blow off other tasks that hold a lot more priority.

In this instance, you'll want to be disciplined enough to know that saying no to these tasks is fine. It won't be the be all to end all. Also, you'll want to learn the words "not now" in terms of those not urgent but important tasks.

The truth is you need to pay close attention to your most critical tasks (your urgent AND important tasks). The last thing you want to ever do is pull a slight amount of attention and time away from it. Do it once and you'll be sucked into the vortex of doing something else that holds little to no priority over the task at hand.

Use the Eisenhower Matrix to place your most critical tasks in the URGENT and IMPORTANT quadrant first while planning out the day. Then schedule the URGENT and NOT IMPORTANT next, followed by NOT URGENT but IMPORTANT last.

THE TENDENCY TO OVERTHINK AND IMAGINE THE WORSE

Ah yes. Overthinking. If that isn't one of the most serious symptoms of doing nothing, we don't know what is. But what exactly causes overthinking?

Believe it or not, there are a few things that overthinking can stem from. Let's cut to the chase and identify them:

- **Past mistakes:** People make mistakes. That's just the undeniable truth. But the real problem is because of them, most people are afraid to do something again. They fear that they'll mess up on something and it will turn out less than perfect. They fear failure (and deem it as an opportunity to give up and move one).

- **You play the same scene in your head repeatedly:**
  Suppose you have a presentation coming up. This is the big
  one where you land a big client if you succeed. And if you
  make one mistake, it will cost you. The "what ifs of things
  gone wrong" tend to pop up. It's okay to practice and
  rehearse the presentation to iron out the wrinkles. In fact,
  overthinking will suck up plenty of time that should
  otherwise go towards rehearsing your presentation. And if
  you make a mistake, don't make a big deal out of it. Act as if
  it never happened and move on.

- **You focus on the "worst case scenario":** Visualization
  is a great preparedness tool. And there is nothing wrong
  with it. However, visualizing the worst that could happen
  will mentally overpower you to a point where fear of failure
  will settle in. Instead of focusing on the worst, focus on the
  best-case scenario. The more you visualize it and practice it,
  the better off you'll be. Also, don't worry about perfection.
  Just rehearse as if you are going through the motions.

- **Worrying about things beyond your control:**
  Everybody worries about things. Especially when it's things
  they can't change nor control. It's not your fault that a nasty
  thunderstorm knocked out power and left the city in the
  dark. Nor is it your fault if some dastardly cyber villain hacks
  into the computer network at the office, which also
  complicates things in the process. Another thing beyond
  your control is someone else's decision making. You can
  persuade someone to make a decision to an extent. However,
  if they don't follow through then don't worry about it. It's

their decision and you can't blame them for it. On the bright side, it could be the worst decision they've made, and they'll come to regret it sooner rather than later.

WHY OVERTHINKING IS BAD

If you think overthinking is some kind of minor thing, you'd actually be surprised. Overthinking may place a negative role in your mental psyche. In fact, it could trigger mental illnesses that may cause you to lose your sanity and peace of mind.

Not only that, but overthinking will make problem solving even harder. It can even make solving the most basic problem that can be solved in five seconds even more complex. It's hard to imagine that ever happening to someone.

Last but certainly not least, it can also affect your sleep patterns. It's good to have a sharp and clear mind when you are well rested. But overthinking will be the biggest obstacle in making that happen.

It will turn what could otherwise be 7 to 9 hours of sleep into 3 to 4 hours. And that's the last thing you want to deal with any day of the week.

How to "kill" your overthinking

So, how do you go about dispatching your overthinking with extreme prejudice? What you may not know is that there are simple solutions. Here are some things we highly recommend you do to ensure that overthinking is a thing of the past:

Know what you can control and what you can't: Accepting the fact that you can't change or control the things that are beyond you is what you need to do. Things that are not directly associated with you will always happen. It's always good to be prepared to be slightly ahead of the curve when things go south.

For example, if you are doing a PowerPoint presentation, have some hard copies handy in the event of the computer you use mysteriously dying. Just shrug it off as another one of those things that you can't control, hand the people you're presenting the hard copies and lead them in a follow along. Not only will they be impressed with how you handled such a situation, but they will love that someone took the initiative to stay ahead of Murphy's Law.

Optimism is key: If you fail, it won't be the end of the world. Think to yourself that one day, there will be a favorable outcome. That one day could come tomorrow, six months from now, or next year. It will happen. Don't let failure be the end all to be all.

Cheer for yourself: It's easy for us to be hard on ourselves. But that will really embed some negative seeds in your mindset. Instead, you can be your own best cheerleader. Even if no one believes in what you can do, you are your best believer. And that alone sets you a head above shoulders over those who don't think this way.

Learn to meditate: There is nothing more satisfying than meditation. No, you don't have to close your eyes and chant "omm" every minute. You can do it quietly in a separate space where no one can bother you. We also would be remiss if we didn't suggest any guided meditation apps like Calm or Headspace. Also, some guided meditation videos on YouTube will always come in handy. You could also incorporate it in your daily routine. It doesn't have to be long. Just block off five minutes of your day and try it out.

With your ability to eliminate overthinking with little to no effort, you have one of the key skills that will no doubt set you apart from those who lack discipline and mental toughness. Restraining yourself from negative thoughts and self-doubt is a powerful skill that will show through your body language and the way you behave.

There is no tricking your subconscious. If you have a positive inner mindset and you train your brain not to overthink, people will know a mentally strong and self-disciplined individual without even asking a single question.

JUST ADMIT IT, YOU DON'T LIKE RESPONSIBILITY

We're not trying to sound rude or anything. A lot of us are not huge fans of responsibility. And you are more than likely one of them.

Just know that you are not alone in this sentiment. People hate being able to own up to things. And that's where it's easy to blame others even though you know deep down that you're at fault.

People seem to avoid responsibility like the plague. Responsibility itself is like a bloodhound. It doesn't matter how much you shake it off, it will hunt you down and find out where you're hiding soon enough. So, you might as well take on responsibilities when the opportunity presents itself.

Learning how to take responsibility for things must be taught at an early enough age. Being responsible will help strengthen your wellbeing, your decision making, and how productive you can be. On top of that, responsibility will also help you strengthen yourself in times when you'll be making certain decisions.

Specifically, these are decisions that won't go over well with others. But they are the kind of decisions that will be for a greater good. For example, you're an executive who is faced with the responsibility of laying off one of two people due to cutbacks.

You know that making such a decision can save the company money. However, your decision may decide the fate of someone who has been a loyal and dedicated employee for a number of years. It will alter the course of their life for the long term.

You need to swallow hard, make a choice, and move forward.

Why no one wants to be held liable

Being held liable may sound like a legal term. Yet, in this context we are discussing liability in terms of what happens when the outcome is negative. There isn't a single person alive who would want a negative outcome.

They happen all the time. But the real issue lies in how one person will handle it. Will they handle the negative outcome with optimism and treat it like a learning lesson? Or will they lay blame on something or someone knowing full well the outcome may have been well in their control?

There are a few reasons why people do the latter: one, they are afraid of failure. Or in plain English, they don't know how to handle it properly. Second, they are not confident in their abilities. And lastly, they choose not to be involved in as much of the process as possible.

So, they decide to hang back behind the scenes and do nothing for fear that if things go wrong, it's their fault. Inaction will earn you a share of the blame, so avoiding liability won't help you.

The fear of failure or lack of confidence will serve as an excuse. The doing of a task will be enough to help you gain the confidence in going forward next time, whether you fail or not. And once again, failure is not the be all to end all.

If you give it your best and it results in the negative, it's important to take a look at what went wrong, discuss what could have been done differently, and move on. Also, people will blame you for the failure (which you shouldn't take personally). People who blame others is a sign of the inability to handle failure on their own accord.

The inability to handle failure and place blame on others will affect the overall morale and mentality of others. That will make it hard for a group to work together on future projects or the like. Learn how to handle failure together if such a thing occurs.

The "diffusion of responsibility"

In a team setting, there may be someone who might be blindly following orders or instructions without knowing what it all entails. That person will usually stand idle and wait for someone to make a move. This is known as the "diffusion of responsibility".

The person who does this needs to take action without waiting for someone else to make the move. Not only that, but it places the other team members in a pressure situation where someone has to make the move. Don't let any lack of initiative come down to that.

The "Yes" Syndrome

It's always a good idea to know your limits. You'll want to learn how to say "yes" to the right responsibilities. On top of that, you'll need to learn how to take on things one at a time rather than overload yourself.

Overloading yourself with responsibilities will overwhelm you. And you may freeze up as a result. You'll begin to panic, overthink, and worry more about what needs to get done first.

This alone will throw everything into chaos. You will soon lose track of what needs to get done. And it will mentally burn you out.

Do not do this to yourself. Know what you are capable of and perform your responsibilities accordingly. Don't feel pressured to say "yes" to all of them.

Learn to say "no", explain your reason why (and make it a good one), and move on.

UNBEKNOWNST TO YOU, YOU'VE ALREADY DEVELOPED FALSE HOPE SYNDROME

Remember that surprise we mentioned earlier on in the chapter? Well, here it is. Whether you know it or not (and it's likely the latter), you already developed what is known as false hope syndrome.

To give you a prime example of this in action, let's talk about New Year's Resolutions. Every year, we vow to make a change for a greater good. It can be losing weight, making more money, quitting smoking, or whatever else.

The real problem is that we fail to fulfill this resolution. Why is this exactly? There is no specific goal that is set. Not to mention, it's lacking in structure.

It's easy for us to adopt the old "go big or go home" mentality. Yet, a lot of us don't seem to know how to set small, tangible goals to get to a much larger one. So instead of "losing weight", just say you're planning on losing 20 pounds.

Then you can outline how to get there. You'll have small milestone goals that you can attain throughout the year. And there is also one thing to keep in mind, set the goals you want to achieve based on your own values.

You're probably scratching your head at that last part. Let's explain it in better detail. Let's say for instance, you want to quit drinking soda or coffee. But there is one thing that stands in your way.

You place a high value on caffeine, which helps you stay awake and alert. Getting rid of coffee or soda will cause you to cut off one of the things you value most. And depriving yourself of things that are personally valuable to you will lead to eventual failure (and giving up your resolutions even before the old groundhog pops up and checks for his shadow).

When settling your goals, consider how it will affect your personal values. If caffeine is really that important, you'll want to explore alternatives that will ensure you still get the caffeine you need without having to resort to anything unhealthy.

If you drink a copious amount of soda on a regular basis, consider cutting that out of your diet. Instead, drink coffee or caffeinated tea. If it's difficult to give up on soda, consider diet or sugar free options. Making changes without hurting your values is possible.

Figure out what is standing in the way

If you are looking for a way to reach a goal or resolution, it's all about identifying the obstacles that stand in the way. Let's say you had a new year's resolution and you failed to fulfill it. What happened? What stood in the way?

Furthermore, ask yourself what you could have done differently. For example, let's circle back to the weight loss goal. You want to spend time working out, so you decide to at least try and do it in the morning before work.

However, you find that your window of time isn't enough, so you give up on it and blame it on a lack of time. Instead of doing that, you should consider blocking off a specific period of time. Why not work out after the workday? It can be as simple as going home, lifting and swinging a kettlebell for 15 to 20 minutes and calling it a day.

Know your values and stay true to them

Your values can either work together or work against each other. That's another reason why people find giving up their goals and resolutions easily. It's important to know what they are and stay true to them as much as possible.

You'll also want to try and mitigate any potential clashes as much as possible. Losing weight while eating to handle stress is counteractive to your goals. So, find an alternative to handle and alleviate stress. Believe it or not, working out is a great stress blaster if we say so ourselves.

Plus, you can use that stress as an energy source to put in the work without killing yourself. You'll feel good knowing that you've utilized that stress to your advantage and decided to knock out some calories in the process. You'll be a lean mean machine that is mentally tough, disciplined, and has a fool-proof way to handle stress when the going gets rough.

Will you always be working out every time you're in a stressful situation? Not always. So, it's important to find other stress management techniques as well.

As long as it's within your own personal values and the results don't counteract with the benefits, you should be in good shape.

YOU END UP DOING SOMETHING ELSE AND YOU STILL KEEP ON JUSTIFYING YOUR ACTIONS

When we end up doing one thing or another, it's easy for us to justify our actions. We make mistakes and we try to explain why we did them. Self-justification is a little more dangerous than any of us would imagine.

We defend our actions or mistakes as if it were one of those "I had to do what was best" moments. It's easy for us to make excuses when we can't give ourselves a straight answer (or to anyone else for that matter).

If you screw up on something and it can be salvageable, the best time to start is right now. Don't wait until tomorrow, next week, or next month. If you screw up and you have an opportunity to start over, jump on it at the earliest time possible (which obviously is now).

One of the top killers for self-discipline is making excuses for yourself. The only way you can stop making excuses is to own up to your mistakes, promise yourself to do better, and say that it can be done.

Self-justifying our actions is equivalent to defending someone who committed a heinous act (even though you know they did it). How can someone you look up to as a mentor be a good person when behind closed doors, they are abusive to their spouse? How can someone be a good person in the face of the public but in private, they are plotting to exploit and scam the same people out of their hard-earned money?

There is no such thing as doing wrong and making yourself look good in the process. This is one of the sure signs of someone who is lacking in discipline and mental toughness. Try as they may, once their house of cards finally falls, they have no choice but to cower in fear and never be seen or heard from again.

Justifying procrastination

Here's the thing with procrastination: you put off something that can be done today, but you'll do it tomorrow. One of the things that is usually said to justify this behavior is "I've got plenty of time throughout the day. I'll do it later". Thus, they'd rather invest their time on other things they think are important all while that time window of doing that exact task is shrinking fast.

Sure, a project that's due two weeks from now is plenty of time. But the sooner you get it done, the better. That way, you can use that spare time to focus on other things or relax (assuming there's nothing else).

NARCISSISTS: LACKING ONE THING, BUT NOT THE OTHER

If someone continues to justify their actions and repeatedly do the same bad things without shame, then that's a sign of narcissism. Here's a plot twist that will shock you: believe it or not, while narcissistic people tend to do wrong and justify their actions, they are mentally tough themselves.

But we're not teaching you to become narcissistic. They are using this power as a weapon of mass destruction. We're showing you how to use it for a greater good.

You see, narcissists use mental toughness to shield themselves from the negativity generated from the people they knowingly hurt and harm. They justify and explain their actions as if it were the right thing (when in reality they know they're wrong). But they don't care.

They lack discipline, but they don't care either. Despite the fact they are mentally tough, they are undisciplined. They will refuse to own up to their mistakes and will place the blame on others.

Lucky for you, this book does give you the keys to being a self-disciplined and mentally tough individual. Unlike the narcissists we speak of, you'll be miles ahead of them in terms of owning your mistakes, learning from them, placing the blame on yourself, and moving forward.

This will help you cultivate a positive self-image in the eyes of your friends, family, and colleagues. You can't be mentally tough and undisciplined, nor be disciplined but not mentally tough. It can't be done.

HOW TO "KILL" SELF-JUSTIFICATION

We can make a decision without thinking twice and be faced with dire consequences. For example, you may be a manager of a small business and make decisions based on cutting back due to financial strain. However, you recklessly make such decisions here or there without the knowledge or input of the employees or customers.

Doing this and saying "it's for the benefit of the company" isn't going to win over anyone. So, how do you go about making the right decisions while killing any opportunity at self-justification? Here are some tips to consider in the long run:

Think it over and ask someone: If you are considering making a decision that carries some serious weight, it's important to not jump on it just yet. It's good to take your time, weigh the pros and cons, and find out who it could affect the most. Ask your most trusted friends, members of your family, or your closest colleagues about what you're considering doing. Ask them about the upsides and downsides. It's better to talk it out and find out what would be the best or worst scenario should it go forward.

Surround yourself with the right people: In this context, the right people are those who will have no problem disagreeing with you. When someone disagrees with you on a potential decision, they are more than likely doing you a favor. They could be saving you from making a fatal error that can never be reversed. They'll also aid you in righting the ship before things get worse. If you are in a leadership position, it's never a good idea to be surrounded by people who will say "yes" 100 percent of the time.

Keep your emotions in check: When decisions are made at high levels of emotion, the likelihood of disaster will be even greater. That's why it is important to put together a plan where you'll need to make the most difficult decisions while keeping the levels of emotion as low as possible. In situations where you're negotiating with the other side on a huge deal or when you decide who gets what in your will when you pass away, you'll want to use more logic than emotion.

Don't use self-justification language: "What about" ..." It's legal" ..." I couldn't do it because" ...these are just a sample of self-justification language. It's important you catch on what you say and use an alternative that doesn't put you in a position of justifying a bad decision.

Don't arrive at conclusions early: Before you even know the real facts, don't arrive at a conclusion. When new information arises, you'll be forced to walk back what you say. And it will make you look bad. Plus, it creates the perfect climate for self-justification.

The sooner you own your mistakes, the better: Why lie to yourself? Why lie to others? When you know you've made a mistake, admit it and move forward. Don't drag it out any farther than you have to.

Assess the situation: It's important to assess a certain situation that you find yourself in. Ask yourself what role you played. Also, ask yourself what could have been done to make it better even if someone is to blame for it (including yourself).

Simply put, a true cornerstone of self-discipline and mental toughness is knowing that it's okay to admit to your mistakes. It won't make you a failure and it certainly won't view you in a more negative manner (unlike denying it, blaming others, and moving on). Resist the urge to place the blame on others, self-justifying decisions that were never right to begin with, and acting as if nothing happened and no one got hurt.

YOU ARE NOT TAKING CARE OF YOURSELF

Whether you know it or not, your lack of discipline and mental toughness can take a toll in more ways than one. Specifically, we're talking about your overall physical health. The truth is, a lack of discipline and mental toughness may lead to some not so good decisions.

Sure, it's nice to treat ourselves with a McDonald's combo meal here and there. But eating fast food on the regular will likely do more harm than good. Especially when it's food that is high in fats, sodium, calories, and so on.

But in this context, the question we need to ask ourselves is: Are we taking care of ourselves mentally? The lack of concentration and focus can lead us down some paths that may not allow us to turn back.

If you are consistently lacking concentration and focus, it can be tied to a few factors. For one, a lack of sleep can lead to it. Aside from that, a lack of sleep can also lead to adverse effects on your physical health as well. As we have hinted earlier, a poor diet can do more harm than good.

Eating the wrong foods on a regular basis can also lead to a lack of concentration and focus as well. It would be better for you to consider making some changes in your diet. Anything high in sugar (for example) will give you that temporary energy and high before you crash back down, and you feel tired.

Also, being stressed all the time will lead to health problems as well. When you are stressed, you can forget about concentration and focus. Stress is like a needle that will keep pricking and poking you to a point where it can be very bothersome. That will throw you off course on the tasks at hand and you'll be pulled away to focus on something that's bothering you more than it should.

Believe it or not, there are medical conditions where a lack of focus and concentration can occur (such as ADHD, diabetes, or even depression). It can also be a symptom of something that could be much worse.

(Note: We are not medical professionals. And we are not in the authority to give you sound medical advice. If you lack focus or concentration and suffer other symptoms like severe chest pains, severe headaches, disorientation, or other signs of a serious condition consult a medical professional immediately. While we talk of putting things off until later, doing so in this situation can have fatal consequences).

HOW TO TAKE CARE OF YOURSELF (WHILE REGAINING CONTROL OF YOUR CONCENTRATION AND FOCUS)

Obviously, the key to better focus and concentration is taking care of yourself. In this section, we will give you a short, easy to follow road map on how to place yourself on the right path. These steps are very simple to follow right from the start. But the important part is to stay consistent and stick with it as much as possible.

Here's what you need to do:

Get a good night's rest: Shoot for 7 to 9 hours of sleep per night. Power down your electronic devices including your smartphone at least 1 ½ to 2 hours prior to your scheduled bedtime (i.e.: If your bedtime is 10pm, do not use your electronic devices past 8:30 pm).

Reduce caffeine intake: Contrary to popular belief, caffeine may not be your saving grace when it comes to concentration. And it can also serve as a roadblock between you and a good night's sleep. If you do take in caffeine regularly, consider cutting it off at least six to eight hours before your scheduled bedtime (i.e. -- 2pm to 4pm if you go to bed at 10pm).

Switch up your eating habits: Instead of eating a few large meals per day, spread them out. Make them small and frequent. The more you eat, the more sluggish you might feel later on in the day. Also, you'll want to incorporate a good amount of fruits, veggies, whole grains, and lean proteins in your diet.

Reduce your stress levels: Stress can really do a number on your concentration. So, you'll need to find ways to go about reducing it even if you have limited time to yourself. Consider some brief meditation sessions. If you have enough time, you can read a book or write in a journal. In the event of the latter, write what's bothering you. Write about what you could have done differently throughout the day, so you are better prepared.

Just so we are clear, we don't want to overwhelm you with the idea of doing all these things at once. But you need to start somewhere. For example, if you want to get a good night's rest then start there. If you stay up late and want to go to bed earlier, you can gradually adjust the time week by week.

So, if you stay up until midnight and your goal is to go to bed at 10pm, start by going to bed an hour earlier one week. If that's a bit much, scale it back to a half hour instead. Scale it back by 30 to 60-minute increments per week until you reach the desired goal.

Remember, you want to make sure you still get seven to nine hours of sleep per night. And you want to know your cutoff times in terms of caffeine and using electronics. You'll be well-rested even if you follow a consistent sleep schedule.

THE LACK OF WILLPOWER, PERSEVERANCE, AND DEDICATION

In this section, we're going to talk about willpower, perseverance, and dedication. Each word will be defined and explained quickly in detail. It's important to have these three abilities on your journey towards self-discipline and mental toughness. Without them, the journey will be impossible to continue.

Willpower Defined And Explained

Willpower has multiple definitions. Yet, no matter what definition you read it will contain the same language. You will hear words like drive, self-control, self-discipline, and so on. Willpower is designed to help you restrain yourself from temptations (albeit for the short-term). The purpose is to ensure that you meet your long-term goals whatever they are.

If not for willpower, humanity would not have survived. Our ancestors had to rely on it in order to survive. We used it to hunt for food, take care of our families, and avoid any external threats to our livelihood. Now, here we are thousands of years later and it seems like it may not matter to most of us anymore.

The truth is that those with a higher level of willpower are usually happier, healthier, and able to manage stress in various situations. The question is: are we born with willpower or do we have to build on it like everything else? Believe it or not, the answer is yes...but to an extent.

Every person is born with willpower. And it can be built up like a muscle. If you are lacking in it, you can find ways to build on it and make it stronger. Like going to the gym, it will take time, commitment, and discipline to make it a complete success.

Willpower is also a test of patience and being able to restrain yourself. For example, let's take a look at an experiment known as the "Marshmallow Test". This was an experiment conducted by Walter Mischel, a psychologist at Columbia University.

Mischel administered the "Marshmallow Tests" to preschool aged children by placing a plate of marshmallows on the table. A child would sit at the table with the plate in front of them. Next, the child would be given the following instructions:

- The researcher administering the test told the child they would leave the room for a few minutes. If they waited for the researcher to return, they could take two marshmallows.
- If the child can't wait, they can ring the bell in front of them. Once the bell rings, the researcher will reappear and instruct them to take only one marshmallow.

Those who waited for the two marshmallows showed they had more willpower than the children that didn't. Years after the research was conducted, it was discovered that those with more willpower had higher SAT scores and a better body mass index (BMI).

The lack of willpower can lead to such links like poor academic performance and poor health. But it doesn't always have to be that way. You can reverse this just by building up on it.

Perseverance: What is it and how to use it

Perseverance is simply defined as doing the task at hand even if there are difficulties in the way. A prime example of this is when you are running a marathon and you are dealing with quite the headache. It makes you want to throw up and maybe even give up when you have a few miles left to go.

But you want to finish the race. You've trained for a year to get this far. So why let that all go to waste now? That is perseverance.

You have something planned out. But you know that there will be difficulties (and some surprises) along the way. It's important for you to be prepared and be able to tackle those obstacles so you can press on and finish the task.

If you are working on a group project, setbacks like people quitting (leading to being shorthanded) can happen. But it can be possible to get the job done with one less person (especially if they haven't pulled their weight).

When building up self-discipline and mental toughness, it will be a challenge right from the start. It will feel uncomfortable and rather painful. Because it's something that you are not used to on a daily basis. Remember, you'll also be making some sacrifices (but are worth the cost since they give you no "return on investment").

No matter how uncomfortable or "painful" it gets, you will want to press on. You've planned on attaining a goal and you took the initiative to start on it. If you've worked on it and make some progress, the last thing you want to do is wipe it all out just by quitting. Not only will it be a waste of time on your part, but it could be a waste of time for others (assuming it's a group project or goal you are working on).

When your back is against the wall and you have setback after setback, it's possible to achieve the task at hand no matter what. Your perseverance will set the stage towards disciplining yourself and developing a rock-hard mental toughness that will be hard to match. You are restraining yourself from taking the easy way out (and giving up).

Remember, giving up will have long term effects. One thing would be dwelling on the "what might have been". What if you didn't give up? What would happen if you did it differently?

Businessman (and two-time presidential candidate) Ross Perot said it best: "Most people give up when they're about to achieve success. They quit on the one-yard line. They give up at the last minute of the game, one foot from a winning touchdown."

In other words, perseverance will put you over the finish line. When you are tempted to give up despite everything thrown your way, don't do it. You may be a lot closer to achieving mental toughness and discipline than you realize.

Dedication: Why It Matters

Dedication is a synonym for commitment. To be dedicated to something, you are committed to getting the job done. You will settle for nothing less. When you are dedicated to something, you have an unmatched passion and loyalty to your mission, and you do not apologize for it.

Being dedicated to achieving discipline and mental toughness may be tough for most. But doing every little bit will put you a head above shoulders over those that don't do anything at all. All it takes for you is to take one step closer and you are miles ahead. However, it's important to not stop and resist the urge of quitting.

When it comes to developing mental toughness, it can be fueled by dedication. You could be dedicated to yourself or something that is a greater cause. Either way, it's important that you stay committed. You can develop mental toughness and stay dedicated even if you decide to take baby steps and not so many giant ones. As long as you take your time and stick to the plan, you're golden.

RECAP

The one person that stands in your way in terms of being more disciplined and mentally tough is you. It's important for you to plan and prioritize your day. The first thing you'll want to knock out are your most critical tasks. The sooner it's done, the better.

Don't worry about the tasks that are not so urgent or important. If a task is urgent, but doesn't hold a lot of importance, consider delegating the task to someone willing to get it done for you. Also, do not worry about the tasks that don't need to be done right away. There will come a time when you will take care of it. And last, don't do anything that will waste a lot of time (which can be otherwise invested in other things).

Overthinking can paralyze you. And it will lead you to not taking the necessary steps to achieve your goals. Figure out what's causing you to overthink. Come to the realization that there are things that will happen well beyond your control. If that happens, find a way to handle it to where it doesn't stress you.

It's true that we are no fans of responsibility. We find it easy to blame others for our mistakes and liabilities. Also, some of us tend to wait before someone else makes a move. That alone puts pressure on the other person to do something. Do your part and make the move. Others will follow. You don't have to be in a leadership position per se to take the initiative on something.

False hope syndrome is something that we are born with. But it can be curable. You cure it by setting goals (not resolutions). Outline them into steppingstones. And make sure they are in line with your values. Never let those values clash together or you may find yourself compromising one or the other.

Self-justification may be necessary, but it should be few. But you should never justify your mistakes, nor make an excuse for why you're procrastinating. Excuses are for the mentally weak and undisciplined.

Being a narcissist that carelessly hurts the morale of others while abusing the power of mental toughness will cast a dark shadow on you. And for most who travel down this path, it will be too late for them to turn back. Further proof that one person (i.e. -- themselves) is their own worst enemy.

It's important to own up to your mistakes and be able to move on early. Denying that you made a mistake and trying to justify it will make matters worse. Just move forward, accept your wrongdoing, and remind yourself not to do it again.

Finally, building discipline and mental toughness requires three things: willpower, perseverance, and dedication. They all go hand in hand. You were born with willpower. But it's what you do with it that will separate you among the others.

Perseverance will help you push through no matter how tough things get. And dedication to yourself or a higher cause will help you build the mental toughness that is needed to make perseverance a walk in the park.

3

A WORLD FULL OF DISTRACTIONS

If there is one thing that is lurking on every corner no matter how near or far it is, it's danger. So, what's dangerous to someone's discipline and mental toughness? Distractions.

In today's modern world, distractions are all over the place. And we live right in the middle of it. Whether it's our smartphones, computers, or anything that is designed to get our attention, we tend to drop everything and pay even more attention to it.

Getting distracted will definitely fuel us to procrastinate more and focus on the less important things. Distractions have the power to "charm" us into how awesome it is to pay attention to them. It will get to the point where it lulls you into a trance and suddenly, you're hooked. Before you know it, hours have passed, and you still haven't done anything that needs to be done.

In this chapter, we'll be delving into distractions and how you can minimize them in your working environment. We'll also show you how to ensure that your relationship with others is helpful in your life and not the other way around. We'll also discuss the Hawthorne Effect and how you can use it to your advantage.

Let's tune in and get right to the chapter:

TAKE A GOOD LOOK AT EVERYTHING AROUND YOU

There's a potential distraction here. Another one there. A distraction across from you.

When you take a good look around you, there's a more than likely chance that there will be something that will distract you. Nine times out of ten, your phone might be within an arm's reach (so there's one potential distraction). Simply put, a distraction is defined as something designed to take your attention off the original task at hand so you can focus on the distraction itself.

Believe it or not, distractions exist in two types: external and internal. External distractions like your phone can be accessed at a moment's notice. On top of that, they can pop up out of nowhere whether it's three feet away or across the street.

Meanwhile, internal distractions will be all in your mind. You're stressed out, tired, or you have a thousand different things rushing through your head that you can't seem to quell. Dealing with these distractions will be a lot harder (but we'll show you how).

Simply put, distractions are all over the place. And the closest they can get to you is inside your mind. In other words, you'll never be too far away from one no matter where you are in the world. Distractions come in all different shapes, sizes, and forms.

Social media for example is a digital distraction. It can form in the shape that fits on your phone or computer screen. And there is all kinds of information that you can access from a social media platform alone. It deserves the top title of being the archenemy of discipline.

Social media may seem like it was designed for a greater good. For people to connect with friends and family. To keep informed about what's going on around them. The truth is that it winds up being one of the most ultimate distractions in existence.

Does it mean that you should get rid of social media period? It's your call. But it's a matter of limiting your use at times when you need to focus. When the task at hand needs a serious investment in time and attention, perhaps it's time to put away any distractions that may be within reach.

Believe it or not, excessive use of social media is not just a sign of being undisciplined. It also signals the possibility of depression and anxiety. The feeling of being wanted or appreciated. No, not everyone who uses social media is that way. But we can correlate social media use to not just a lack of discipline but also a lack of mental toughness.

One truth you might not realize is that our brains were made to distract us. Then again, you may not be surprised considering the fact we have already talked about internal distractions. You have things that run through your mind. The "what ifs" or the "should haves" are a good example. Also, the amount of information overloading in your brain will certainly distract you.

With all the information overload, you might end up opening up multiple tabs on your favorite web browser without thinking twice. And believe us when we say that this happens all the time. But if you can teach your brain to be less of a distraction and more of a weapon for positive thought and focus, only then it will serve you well in the long run.

CLEANSE YOUR WORK ENVIRONMENT OF DISTRACTIONS

In a work environment, distractions exist. As mentioned before, it doesn't matter where you are there's always going to be one closer than you think. It's important to consider cleansing your work area of these distractions as much as possible.

It may seem hard to do at first. But once you get the hang of it, it will be like second nature. In this section, we'll share with you our favorite tips on working more while getting less distracted. Distractions will be one of the major roadblocks towards discipline and mental toughness. With that in mind, here are some tips to consider:

Dispatch your technological distractions FIRST: With modern technology being one of the largest sources for many distractions, it's important that we start off with what we can do to minimize the distractions on our devices. If you are working on a computer, you should consider the idea of activating a blocker. There are plenty of blocking apps that you can run while you are in the process of working on something. You can use it to block social media apps and websites like Facebook or Twitter (if you use Google Chrome, there are some extensions that you can use like Cold Turkey). Don't think for a moment that your web browser is the only source for distraction. There's also your smartphone.

It's easy for us to take our phone out of our pockets the second we hear that notification sound go off. Before we know it, we're texting, commenting, tweeting, and so on. One of the things you should do is put the phone on airplane mode or "do not disturb" mode. This will allow your phone to stifle any notifications for as long as it's activated. One more thing you need to do is place your phone in a different part of the room.

If your workspace is inside your house, put it in a different room like a living room or kitchen. If you're in an office setting, put it in a locker or a filing cabinet near you (preferably in one of the cabinets with a lock. Just make sure you have the key before you accidentally lock it and can't get to it).

Focus on your most time sensitive and critical tasks first:

Your most time-sensitive and critical tasks must be done as soon as possible. Failure to do so will lead to quite a bit of chaos. Not to mention, these tasks can be hard to do when the pressure is on and timing is not in your favor. You should focus on the first two or three critical tasks of the day first before doing anything else. One critical task may also be enough before moving on to the others. Either way, the more you get out of the way the better.

Use minimums to your advantage: What would you do? 50 pushups a day or 5? If you answered 5, good choice. Doing the minimum amount of work rather than focus on something larger will help you get in the mindset of doing little but ending up going a little beyond that. So, if the goal is 5 pushups, you may feel inclined to do more work. From there on, you'll be able to up your minimums to a point where you can do a bit more without breaking a sweat (or your mind). The minimum is a baby step closer to the ultimate goal. Do the minimal amount, take a break, then do it again.

Eliminate any sources of internal distractions: Internal distractions can and will occur at any time. You could be stressed. You could be tired. Or maybe even both. The solutions we provide are probably some you've heard of before. Get a good night's rest the night before. Meditate for five minutes before you begin the day's work. Anything that can be proven to minimize stress can work to your advantage. Just remember, internal distractions are just as bad as the external ones. If you can't get rid of them outright, find ways to minimize them as best you can.

Run a visualization through your head: Before every big game, an athlete will visualize their success. Nine times out of ten, it works to perfection. You can do this yourself. Imagine yourself working on the tasks at hand without stress or with the feeling that nothing can stop you. Take a few minutes to ponder on it. If you can visualize it, it can certainly give you the confidence to get it done. Another visualization technique is to reverse engineer your accomplishment. In other words, start backwards from the end to the beginning. Visualize your actions in small steps.

Minimize external distractions: This one might be a lot easier than dealing with the internal distractions. This could mean moving to a quieter area, putting on headphones with your favorite music or binaural beats, or just putting away your phone or devices. The more external distractions you can identify, the better. Find ways to minimize them or temporarily eliminate them until the work is done.

Keep the momentum going: When you have all your distractions tuned out, you'll have a clear path to accomplishing the task at hand. You work at least on the bare minimum, take a quick break, and repeat. It's all about focusing on that one thing, putting the pedal to the medal and never looking back. Distraction can be a momentum killer. Just remember to focus on the small things, nothing too big and crazy.

YOUR RELATIONSHIP WITH OTHERS SHOULD HELP YOU, NOT SABOTAGE YOU

Relationships in your life are not a burden to you and your goals. So, they shouldn't be considered an outright distraction. However, there is work to be done. So how do you go about achieving your goals and minimizing distractions without upsetting those who are most important to you?

We can sum this up in one word: communication. There is no such thing as the perfect work/life balance. There are days when the workday can require you to put in extra time. Will it cut into time that will otherwise be spent on your significant other or family? Unfortunately, yes. But the good news is it's a lot less than you think.

Family will always come first no matter what. This is something you want to reiterate with them when you are communicating with them. If there is some kind of major project coming up where it requires your time and attention, you need to make them aware of it. Let them know that there will be times when you'll be home late and there may be limited time you can spend with anyone (since you're going to need your rest).

Tell them that you are not ignoring them (nor forgetting about them). After all, let your family know that they are the reason why you have the drive to work hard. The most important people in your life are your best cheerleaders. They inspire you to better yourself when others will not. Even if no one else will support you, they will. They are your closest allies when the going gets tough.

When relationships become distractions

Another thing you want to do is evaluate your relationships outside of your family. Are most of the people that you associate yourself with more positive or negative? If you are dealing with negative people in your life, they will end up being a distraction. Lucky for you, you'll have a good idea of keeping that distraction at bay. You can give them less attention or cut them out completely if they are too toxic.

Those who understand what your line of work is and the important things you need to focus on will likely develop a positive relationship with you. They see distraction as a negative thing and will respect your privacy when you need it. Neediness is a distraction within itself. Plus, it's also a two-way street.

For example, someone will need to see you or talk to you. And there are those who need to communicate with someone because they are unhappy, alone, or what have you. Neediness is something you can't deal with or have in your life. When relationships become distractions, the first thing you need to do is minimize it as much as possible. If it gets too bad, cutting out the distractions without thinking twice is something you can do without shame.

Building your support system is key

When focusing on tasks that need to be completed, it's good to have a support system in place. People like your family and friends should be a part of it. However, they need to realize that when things get busy, they will give you their full-throated support and leave it at that so you can focus. They won't bother you nor will they doubt you in getting the job done.

A support system doesn't have to be ridiculously large. You can build it with a few like-minded friends, and it can be stronger than steel. Don't be afraid to reach out to people that you want to be a part of it either. It's good to vet people who you want as your most trusted allies. Plus, it can be a tough, but rewarding task.

Strengthen and maintain your relationships

Relationships are a two-way street. One person does their part to keep it strong and well maintained. You return the favor (and vice versa). It can't be where one person is solely responsible for building it. Remember, communication is the key to a strong and healthy relationship. Without it, there's nothing that either party will bring to the table.

One more thing, aside from regular communication you want to build the relationship by building value while expecting nothing in return. If you try to grovel or the like, then people will be well aware of ulterior motives you might have.

USE THE HAWTHORNE EFFECT TO YOUR ADVANTAGE

Next, we'll be discussing what is known as the Hawthorne Effect. What exactly is it? It's named after an experiment that was conducted almost a hundred years ago. It was believed that when someone was being watched or the central part of someone's focus, they would perform their tasks (and with great effectiveness). It's almost as if they don't want them to fail in front of anyone.

While someone might not literally be watching you while you work, you want to act as if someone is watching your every move. Your boss will always keep tabs on employees who are hired to do the work. If you deliver the work as expected, then you are rewarded. If you do nothing, your boss will notice that you are not pulling your weight. You may be reprimanded or terminated from your job.

If you are part of a group project, you are being watched for doing your part. Rest assured, everyone in your group is watching each other so everyone is on the same page and fulfills their responsibilities. If it's in a school setting, they know that the grade they get as a group will either benefit or hinder their overall economic performance.

People perform better and will get the task done if they know they are being watched. For example, there was one research experiment done where medical staffers were the subject. When watched, the staffers were 55 percent more likely to wash their hands and comply with safety precautions compared to those not being watched.

As mentioned, it's easy to make mistakes and do little work when you are not being watched. Just because you're not being watched all the time, it doesn't mean that you should slack off. There will come a time when you may be subject to some kind of random accountability check. It's important to follow deadlines and get the most important tasks done at every opportunity you have. You'll want to approach each task as if you will be evaluated on it after completion.

The Hawthorne Effect will make it so that accountability partners are much needed than ever. That way, you hold each other accountable for whatever tasks you may perform. The lack of accountability can lead to a decline in productivity not just for yourself but also your partner. It's important to find someone you can trust to hold you accountable while they do their own part.

ENHANCE YOUR FOCUS AND UNPLUG REALITY

In a world full of distractions, it is absolutely paramount to make sure that your focus is better than ever. Sometimes, it's always a good idea to disconnect yourself from reality for a few hours just so you can focus. One of the best ways to go about increasing your focus is going on a digital detox.

A digital detox is defined as pulling yourself away from social media or even digital devices. This can be done every day simply by not hopping on social media or looking at your phone for a few hours. Some will even take on the challenge of going without social media for days, weeks, or even months. It all comes down to willpower.

THE BENEFITS OF A DIGITAL DETOX

If you have never done a digital detox, then you may want to consider doing one. Below is a list of benefits that you may enjoy should you go forward with the idea. A lot of people try to do one but quickly give up (a recurring theme for most of us). And it goes back to the value of feeling connected to other people. However, there is a benefit that will make you feel more connected to the people you appreciate even more.

Let's take a look at the list of benefits now:

1. Improved connection with other people

It's no secret that cell phone use can be a burden on human interaction. At least 82 percent of Americans will share that sentiment. That's why it's always a good idea to keep your phone in your pocket and on vibrate while you are spending quality time with family or with your friends. It's a lot better to have a fulfilling conversation or have a ton of fun without the use of any digital devices.

The last thing you want to do is dig out your phone while talking to the other person. The latter will feel ignored. They will feel like they don't provide you with enough personal value. Sometimes, there may be that piece of information stuck in your head where you subconsciously dig out your phone to look it up without even thinking.

Instead of looking it up mindlessly, you can mention bringing it up in the form of a question during your conversation (if you feel that it's relevant). If not, make a mental note to look it up online later.

2. Reduces stress

Did you know that technology is a source of stress? Yep. Technology can go haywire or someone may say something on the Internet that is outright ridiculous. Either way, something about technology will stress someone out. It's important for you to refrain from long-term use. The person who spends an hour a day on their phone will be less stressed than someone who spends a few hours per day.

3. You'll sleep better

Electronics emit a blue light that can reduce natural melatonin levels. Melatonin is a chemical that helps you sleep at night. That's why it is important to shut down any electronics at least an hour and a half or two hours prior to bedtime (as we've mentioned early on in the book). Not only does better rest help you sleep, but it's also a building block in reducing amounts of stress. Better sleep and a digital detox go hand in hand. The next benefit will explain why.

4. Better focus and concentration

A good night's rest and a digital detox will give you a better chance at having more focus and concentration throughout the day. You don't feel distracted in the slightest. Also, your attention span will increase four seconds in length compared to the average person. Believe it or not, the average person's attention span is a mere eight seconds. To have a twelve second attention span will set you a head above shoulders over the rest.

5. Increased problem-solving skills

When there's a problem and the digital distractions are not consuming you whole, you will be more alert and aware of the problem. And it will also help you use your brain by thinking a little deeper. It will also help you recall things better than those who have to rely on modern technology.

6. You'll be a lot happier

It's widely known that those who are highly dependent on social media and technology will likely have some kind of depression. But a digital detox for a few hours or even long-term (days or weeks) can improve your happiness considerably. You will be able to have a vested interest in doing activities that you'll enjoy more. Not to mention, they will be a bit more focused on that task rather than retreating back to their digital device.

Logging off social media and the Internet in general will more than likely improve your level of happiness (even for the long-term). On top of that, your levels of anxiety will be reduced considerably.

HOW TO DO A DIGITAL DETOX

Now that you know the benefits of doing a digital detox, perhaps it's time for you to try it out for yourself. Not only will it be a test of your discipline and mental toughness, but it will give you an opportunity to iron some of life's wrinkles. You may figure out why you're stressed or feeling less than happy in terms of your overall mood. So, with that in mind, let's take a look at some tips that you'll need to take to heart when planning to do a digital detox:

Determine how much time you want to spend: Do you want to go without technology for a few hours a day? Or do you want to go longer? This will depend on how severe the need is. If you're looking at your phone every few minutes and placing a high importance on every notification, you know it's time for a digital detox. To start, you would want to consider starting off slow (about 4 to 6 hours a day) and then gradually working your way up. Once you become comfortable with the idea of going without your devices for longer periods, you can make the adjustments.

Consider alternative activities: What do you want to do instead of looking at your phone? Think about the activities you enjoy doing. Ask yourself, what would you do if you didn't have your phone on hand. Would you read a book? Why not take a walk outdoors?

Consider a cut off time and stick with it: For those who want to do a more scaled back version of a digital detox, it's important to choose a time where you "can't touch" your phone. One prime example is at least an hour and a half to two hours prior to your scheduled bedtime (something we've touched on earlier in the book). When that time comes, you honor that cut off time. Not a second longer.

Shut off notifications: Take a look at the apps that you normally use. There's a pretty good chance that most of your notifications are from your social media apps (Facebook, Twitter, Instagram, etc.). You can shut them off completely or during work hours. Either way, it will work to your advantage.

Say "no" to apps for a week: One of the key aspects of self-discipline is being able to say "no" to things that may be hard to resist. Clearly, your most used apps like social media is one of them. If they are the apps you are planning to shut off for the week, make sure that your friends and family have other alternative forms of contacting you (like phone or email).

Clean out your inbox: How many email newsletters do you subscribe to? We have a habit of letting in so many into our inbox. You have one email in your inbox. Then it goes to ten. Then a hundred. It's so overwhelming you're just trying to keep up. If you're getting pummeled with newsletters and such over the course of the day, your inbox is in need of some serious cleaning. Unsubscribe from email lists that provide no value to you. If they are from an online store you haven't shopped at in the past 60 to 90 days and have no plans to buy there again, unsub from the list.

These are the tips that you want to follow when you want to do a digital detox. It may be hard to say no to your favorite apps for at least a week. And it might be tough to keep away from your phone during the most important hours of the day.

A digital detox is one of the true tests for discipline, willpower, commitment, and most importantly mental toughness. Think of this as the brand-new marshmallow test. Except, you're not waiting on someone to come back. Waiting one week to access Facebook or Instagram again is the challenge.

It will also help you find alternative things to do so your mind is more focused on that than the desire to hop on your phone and post something. Just take it one day at a time and don't focus on the week itself. Start out small and minimal.

RECAP

It's true that the world is full of distractions. Unfortunately, they will still exist all over the place both around you and inside your head. The only thing you can do is minimize them as much as possible.

Your external distractions can be minimized by working in a much quieter area where you are allowed to maximize your focus. Tune out as much of the outside noise as you can. These can be as easy as slapping on a pair of headphones, shutting off your notifications between a specific time period, and being able to program your computer to deny you access to certain websites throughout a period of the day.

Internal distractions also exist. They may be tough to minimize them (not to mention, they will take time). The best ways to deal with them are getting a good night's rest and reducing stress. Believe it or not, there is a solution where you're allowed to do both things (and it's all linked to your use of electronic devices).

It's important for you to stay the course, keep building momentum, and never lose focus. One instance of breaking momentum and you'll fall behind. If you need to take a break, take a five to ten-minute break and prevent using your electronic devices (for obvious reasons).

Your relationships will matter most. They shouldn't be treated like a burden either. These people in your life are your family, close friends, and colleagues. It's true that you need some alone time to focus on your work. But sometimes, you need to be aware that you have a support group consisting of individuals that are all rooting for you.

If anything, they are here to help you push through and hold yourself accountable. Speaking of accountability, that's where the Hawthorne Effect comes into play. You won't have someone watching over you all the time. But those who know of what you can accomplish will be interested in how things are going. Act as if someone is keeping a watchful eye on you at all times (without feeling paranoid).

Lastly, it never hurts to unplug. Doing a digital detox for a short or long-term period can work to your advantage. Not only will you be less distracted, but you'll also find yourself more in tune with your mind. You'll feel happier, more productive, and see things at a different angle compared to most people.

III

UNEARTHING YOUR REASON
TO CHANGE

4

START WITH THE WAY YOU THINK

Most of the challenges you will face in your life will focus more on the mental aspect versus the physical. In sports, they say most of it is 90 percent mental while the physical part is only 10 percent. When it comes to discipline and mental toughness, the same concept pretty much applies.

In this chapter, we'll focus on one part of the mental side of things. It starts with the way you think. It's up to you to adopt a mindset that will allow you to go from undisciplined to disciplined (and mentally weak to tough). We'll define what mindset is and discuss the two types that exist: fixed and growth.

A bit of a spoiler alert: the fixed mindset isn't going to be what you'll want to adopt here. Therefore, we'll be talking about how to adopt the growth mindset and how you'll use it to your advantage on the journey towards being the most disciplined, mentally tough individual on the planet.

If you are looking for a way to bust through the mental blocks but don't know how, this chapter will help you take a wrecking ball to them so you can press on. Let's jump right in and start with the definition of mindset:

Mindset: A way of thinking or a frame of mind.

Yes, the definition is simple and to the point. Don't we wish that switching to a positive mindset was as simple as that? There are two types of mindsets that exist. Let's take a look at them and explain how they work:

Fixed mindset: This kind of mindset is where nothing seems to change. The qualities of which you possess are unchangeable and you're stuck with it forever. However, that's just the definition. But it's possible to change it.

Growth mindset: With this mindset, you can be able to go forward each day with the belief that you can improve and grow. You can grow and strengthen yourself through hard work and dedication. This is the mindset we want you, dear reader, to aim for. Is it impossible to acquire? Only if you think that way.

With a fixed mindset, there's always the fear of being judged and worrying about not living up to someone's expectations. Those with a growth mindset don't care who's judging them. And they could care less about who's expectations they live up to (or don't live up to). If anything, they are focused on the goals they set forth and move forward.

Those with a fixed mindset and a growth mindset are susceptible to making mistakes. Yet, the only difference is they handle them in a different way. Those with a fixed mindset find mistakes to be the "devil's work". So, they try to avoid them like the plague. And it is for this reason they try to become perfectionists. And if you know a perfectionist or two, you notice that they share the common emotion of getting angry when things are less than perfect.

Those with a fixed mindset find mistakes to be a "be all end all thing". And thus, failure means the end of the world. They don't learn from their mistakes and don't bother to take on any other challenges for fear that it would be too tough and complex (thus the fear of failure settles in quickly).

A growth mindset sees things a different way. They know that mistakes happen. They take them as learning lessons, so they don't make the same mistakes again. They don't care about perfection, but they will never settle for anything less than satisfactory. They know that quality matters most in what they do. But as long as they get the task done, they should have no problem.

YOUR MINDSET CAN DICTATE YOUR NEXT WORDS AND ACTIONS

If you think it's hard to tell who has a fixed mindset and who has one that is growth oriented, you may be surprised. In fact, you can hear it in their voice or language. You can see it in their body language if you are very observant. You don't have to be an expert at reading people to know what kind of mindset another person has.

Yet, you'd be hard-pressed to find someone who has more of a growth mindset. Especially, when they have goals that they know they can achieve no matter how long it takes them. But that doesn't mean they are few and far between in the slightest.

You can adopt a mindset of growth if you so choose to do so. And when you do, you'll find yourself speaking in a different way. Instead of saying "I can't", say "I can". Or instead of "if I fail, it's over" you can say "if I fail, I'll learn from it and be ready for next time". It's hard to understand why it's difficult for someone to switch their mindset from fixed to growth.

They say, "fake it until you make it". This may work to your advantage to an extent. Or you can act as if you have already achieved your goal. When you act as if you've accomplished something, you'll feel like you can accomplish the next task with ease. It just might help you on your journey towards adopting a growth mindset.

But one thing to keep in mind is to be congruent. If you are acting that you have a growth mindset but react to something negative in a way someone with a fixed mindset would, then it might be hard to gain trust from people if you seem to be putting up some kind of front. However, you'll want to act as if someone is watching your every move (hello Hawthorne, we meet again).

This means you'll need to push yourself to weather through that negativity. You have no other choice. People are watching and assuming that you have a good mindset. Don't prove them wrong or fool them into thinking otherwise. Not only will it force you into a situation where you can level up on discipline and mental toughness, but you'll soon realize that adopting a growth mindset isn't so bad after all.

THE MINDSET OF A DISCIPLINED AND MENTALLY TOUGH PERSON

So, what exactly does the mindset of a disciplined and mentally tough person look like? In this section, we'll give you an in-depth look. Obviously, they have a growth mindset. But what specifically goes through the mind of someone who is already disciplined and mentally tough? Learn from this section and take notes so you can be able to reverse engineer exactly how to adopt that very mindset from the end to beginning.

A disciplined and mentally tough person is more than likely to embrace challenges whenever they are thrown at them. They know that failure isn't the be all to end all. They are aware of the potential setbacks that can occur. But they are ready for them at any given moment. Once they complete tasks, they are not afraid to receive positive criticism that will better them in the future.

They don't care about the "negative", unsolicited criticism some people tend to give out to make the latter feel bad. A disciplined and mentally tough person will learn from pieces of advice from their mentors before applying it in the future. Depending on their goals, they take a look at people who have already achieved them. They study what they've done, what their setbacks were, and how they overcame them.

They learn the stories about someone's success, and they use it as inspiration to push themselves forward. Now they know who to model their success after, they tailor it to their own approach towards their goals and accomplishments. They know they can achieve a higher level of results. They don't care how long it will take them.

If they achieve it in a short amount of time, good. If it takes a bit longer than average, they'll just shrug it off. At least they got it done and that's all that matters. They will say they had setbacks, but they managed to get through them. They have the determination to push through anything that gets in the way.

Lastly, they know that a lapse in discipline can occur (and yes, it does happen). But when they recognize it, they pick themselves back up and get back on the path. They hold themselves accountable and get straight to work. The Dali Lama said it best:

"A disciplined mind leads to happiness. An undisciplined mind leads to suffering."

— THE DALI LAMA

Those words could not be spoken more truthfully. However, it's hard to adopt since they seem to have the desire to stay ahead and push anyone who stands in the way. However, a disciplined person knows that competition is not their worst enemy. They see a competitor as someone who could be of value to them at some point down the road.

Someone who is self-disciplined enough will stick to the plan. They will stay focused and not make any changes to "keep up" with someone. The whole "keeping up with the Joneses" attitude is a trait of those who are undisciplined. And that alone could lead them to an unhappy life, financial distress, and so on. A mentally disciplined individual doesn't worry about people who have the best things and flaunt them.

Discipline and mental toughness are two things that will help you achieve the best level of happiness. It is your weapon against those who try to buy nice things in order to cover for their insecurities (meanwhile, while triggering the other people to do the same and thus continuing a vicious cycle). Don't fall for the trap of "keeping up" because someone else decides to compensate for their lack of confidence and security.

OVERCOMING THE FEAR WITHIN

Fear is another thing that holds us back from doing anything. Yet, for the person that adopts the growth mindset they know that fear is something that doesn't faze them in the slightest. They are afraid of things going south or some kind of setback. But they just say, "screw it" and get on with the task. Fear will hold you back if you let it.

You will fail. You will feel like crap. But the way you handle it will set you ahead of the others. You may feel embarrassed. But it gives you the energy to learn from your mistakes and move forward. Don't think for a moment that the people who love you most (and are a part of your support system) will lose faith in you if you screw up. It's not like they expect you to get it perfect on the first try.

If anything, fear should be fuel. It should be that energy and drive that will push you to get the work done and earn the reward that is the sense of accomplishment you feel after the fact. Yes, fear is a powerful emotion. But you can be able to convert it into something that will drive you out of your comfort zone and do something different. When you're in your comfort zone, things will be the same old, mundane, boring things. And that will really make you feel like you've done nothing with your life.

Too much comfort and complacency will cause you to miss out on the things that matter most. Meanwhile, if you have a willingness to face fear and stand outside of your comfort zone then there is no sense of waiting for the right moment. That moment to get something done is right now. Restrain yourself from doing what otherwise could be the exact opposite (like doing nothing).

TIPS ON HOW TO HANDLE FEAR

Below is a list of things that you can do in order to handle your fear. This will give you an opportunity to get to know yourself on a much deeper level. You may have some fears that you never knew about. Or you may be afraid of a lesser number of things. Either way, it is important to know your fears and find a way to conquer them.

Here are the following tips to put to good use:

Write down what you're afraid of: First thing you should do is get a piece of paper. Or open up a word document if you feel more comfortable. Spend time thinking about what you're afraid of. The deeper you go into detail, the better. What are your fears? Why are you afraid of it? What can do you to face that fear or at least stop it from getting the best of you?

Realize that you're in control: As the old saying goes, "those who control you, have the power over you". Do you want to live your life knowing that your every fear will control the frame? Or do you want to gain control over fear and use it to your advantage? Letting fear control, you will lead to inaction. And inaction means getting nothing accomplished.

Adopt positive affirmations: Affirmations are a great way to mentally program yourself into what you should believe in. As silly as it may sound, it has actually worked for people. You can say things like "I will not let my fear control me" a few times while looking at yourself in the mirror. You should consider putting affirmations to good use on a regular basis. You can do them in the morning the first thing you wake up and do them again before you go to bed. Either way, they will be helpful in developing your mental toughness.

Visualize yourself facing fear: As mentioned in the book, we suggested visualizing your accomplishment. Another reason why we are so big on it is because we see ourselves getting the job done without fear controlling us. And we imagine ourselves enjoying that sense of accomplishment that rushes through our veins. That feeling can become reality if we say, "to hell with fear", put the pedal to the medal, and get to work. It's better to visualize your accomplishments before getting started rather than visualize about what might have been.

It's okay to talk about them: Your fears aren't something that people will laugh at. If they do, it's more of their problem than it is yours. Talk to someone who you can trust like a member of your family or a trusted friend (especially someone in your support system). Tell them what your plans are and why you're not acting on them due to a certain fear. There's a good chance that they will reassure you that everything will be fine. If you succeed, great. If you fail, don't let it get to you. Opportunities will arise (even if they sound like some kind of once in a lifetime thing).

These tips will help you overcome your fear of whatever it is that may be holding you back from doing anything. Don't let fear restrain you. It should be the exact opposite (which is pretty much one of the main points of this book).

VISUALIZING THE FUTURE AHEAD OF YOU

As mentioned before, visualization will play a huge role in helping you press through fear so you can accomplish your goals. It will also help you along the path towards self-discipline and being able to toughen up mentally. Visualizing the steps you take and the outcome you want to achieve is essential.

How do you go about visualizing your success? What can you do to ensure that things will work to your advantage? We'll be taking a look at some tips below on how you can visualize your success for both the short-term and long-term.

Before we go forward with the tips, it's important to set this one condition: **you need to know what you want.** What is your ultimate goal? What is it exactly that you want?

Without a clear goal in mind, you won't be able to visualize it and be able to go forward in achieving it. Not to mention, you won't have the ability to have the discipline or the mental toughness to make it happen.

Here are some suggestions that we consider effective:

Put together a vision board: Vision boards have grown in popularity over the years. The way these work are as follows: you have a cork board or poster that you can create into a makeshift collage. These are quite inexpensive to put together. And if you see an image that reminds you of your goal, you can always add it onto your vision board. Just one more reminder why the goal you set to achieve is important.

Write in a gratitude journal: A journal is a great way to visualize and write down what you are thankful for. At night, think of five to ten things you are grateful for. You can also write down something about what's been bothering you as of late, what you could have done differently today, and plan for the future so that you are mentally prepared and ready to take on the next phase of your goal.

Meditation: Of course, meditation will work to your advantage if you are looking to change the way you think. Not only will meditation put you in that "in the moment" mindset. But it will also help you bear down and focus on what you need to accomplish. Before you know it, you'll be done with your most critical tasks with a little more time to spare.

Write a "dream check": While it sounds a bit crazy, you can write a "dream check" of an amount of money you want to shoot for in your lifetime. One of the famous examples of this method was done by none other than actor Jim Carrey. Before rising to stardom, he wrote himself a check for $10 million. He dated it for Thanksgiving 1995. He used it as a visualization tool, and it helped him become one of the best comedic actors in the world. Believe it or not, he landed a role that earned him $10 million by Thanksgiving 1995. The point of this is you can write yourself out a "check" for a monetary value that you realistically want to achieve. Put it on your wall and use it as a source to drive you to perform the tasks and goals that you need to get there.

RECAP

Mental blocks can deter you from changing your mindset or serve as some kind of obstacle that you can blow past. Your mindset can change. It is up to you to determine whether or not you have a fixed mindset or one where growth and improvement is possible. The reality is that most people may not be able to make the switch. But if you decide to go from fixed to growth in terms of mindset, you'll be ahead of a lot of people.

It's important to know the mindset of someone who is disciplined and mentally tough. They carry themselves in such a way that it shows in their body language, the way they say things, and how they deal with stress. One way to familiarize yourself with the mindset of a disciplined and mentally tough individual is to reverse engineer what they have done. Start from the end and finish at the beginning. You'll know this mindset backwards and forwards and know how to take the necessary steps to get where you need to be.

Fear will become a mental block that you'll need to bust through as well. It should be viewed as fuel for pressing on and moving forward no matter what the outcome is. It's fine to visualize a positive outcome in the beginning. But it's important to not think too much of it and just focus on getting a certain task done. If the outcome is not what you desired, take a moment to learn about what went wrong and consider the steps you need to take so you can prevent another mistake.

Visualizing the future is a tool that will instill confidence, discipline, and mental toughness. We know what each of us wants. To incorporate the emotions of our visualizations will help us become more effective in our tasks and help us handle stress and adversity wherever it pops up.

Consider the idea of incorporating visualization tools that will help you push you to become more disciplined, mentally tough, and someone who will rise to the challenge and conquer it. Your mind can be a dangerous weapon against adversity and setbacks. Or it can cave under pressure. Either way, it's up to you to make the mindset change to determine what will happen in those situations.

5

ENGINEERING A DISCIPLINED LIFE

A disciplined life is filled with rewards. One of them is the ongoing sense of accomplishment. The fact that you can get the job done without the setbacks and obstacles getting to you can be quite the feeling. This can be you. And if you want that, keep reading this chapter.

In this chapter, we'll be talking about the "new normal" and how you should embrace it going forward. We'll also take a look at how discipline is like a child. Something that you can "birth" and nurture into something that will be a part of you for the rest of your living days. We'll also talk about what a life of a disciplined person looks like.

The nurturing part of discipline will be very important. So, we'll show you how to connect yourself with the right kind of people who share the same mindset and discipline as you do. And lastly, we'll talk about how you should take the proactive approach to ensure that you are a disciplined individual from the morning you get out of bed to the moment you hit your head on the pillow for a good night's rest.

Onward.

EMBRACING YOUR NEW NORMAL

The words "new normal" have been a part of our vocabulary as of late. Especially with the COVID-19 pandemic changing the ball game on how we live, how we do business, and so on. Some of the things we've considered normal have been unceremoniously thrown out the window without warning. Things that could have been possible in a few years' time have now become the "normal" thing to do.

As a mentally tough and disciplined person, the best thing to do is accept and adapt to change. Even in our lifetime, we may need to change the way we live because we have no choice but to do so. For example, you might be a sucker for spicy foods. But you have a health condition that will discourage you from enjoying them. By order of your doctor, you can't have as much as you used to (or never again).

The new normal may seem like a shock to the system to so many. And many will continue asking questions and have few answers to work with. To a disciplined individual, they are nervous about the new normal. But they get through it with a smile on their face knowing that they can take on the challenge. The uncertainty of what's on the other end makes it even more enticing for them to continue forward.

This new normal will be a challenge to many. Those who rise above it will come out on top. Will you be one of them?

GIVING BIRTH TO DISCIPLINE

Discipline is like a child. You give "birth" to it and raise it as your own. It should be a part of your life. A child needs to be well taken care of so it can grow to be strong both in mind and body. The same can be said for your discipline. It should not be abused or neglected in any way. This is how you should view discipline from this point forward. It's important for you to nurture your discipline and watch it grow into something that will make you even tougher mentally and a better person overall.

Is raising a child an easy task? If you're a parent, you already know the answer. It's not as easy as people think. But the rewards are sweet. Your discipline may not be easy to maintain and nurture. But imagine the kind of benefits and rewards you reap in the process. What may seem like a harmless task that you're doing (like procrastinating), it's hurting your discipline in more ways than one.

Being able to discipline yourself and nurturing it will help make things easy to do. You can develop a new skill with ease. You can get the most critical tasks done with more time to spare. You can resist the urge to get sucked into things that are actually a waste of your time. If you let setbacks get to you or get engaged in "time sucking" activities, your discipline will suffer.

The "Motivation" Myth

People say that you should do a certain task when you feel "motivated" enough. The problem is motivation is elusive. If you look for it, it will go in the opposite direction. Most people are mentally focused on searching for it and forgetting about the tasks before them. Before they know it, they waste plenty of time.

If you want to improve your writing, some advise you to work on it whenever you feel motivated. Why not write anyways? Perhaps write a hundred words first thing in the morning. Then the following day, you can up it to about two hundred and work your way up.

The same can be said about losing weight. Why work out if you have the "spare time"? You know you have a block of time that you can carve out and dedicate it to working out regularly. A few days out of the week for an hour might be just what you need. Just find that available time slot and dedicate it to working out.

Lastly, if you are serious about saving money then consider setting aside a specific amount of money each time you earn. In George Clason's "The Richest Man In Babylon", one of the rules is to set aside 10 percent of what you earn. Just take that portion and set it off to the side in a safe or a box. Use it in case of emergencies, not when you want to splurge (another test in willpower and discipline, now that we think about it).

If you need something to get you going, visualization is the key. Circling back to our previous chapter, you can imagine yourself in your ideal situation and instill the emotions that will drive you to get the job done. Visualization is a hell of a lot better than trying to locate that ever elusive motivation, don't you think?

LOOKING AT THE LIFE OF DISCIPLINED PEOPLE

In the previous chapter, we gave you an in-depth look of the mindset of mentally tough people. Now, we'll be taking a glimpse at the life of someone who lives a disciplined life. And we don't have to go too far in depth by discovering the kind of traits they possess. You can tell who is disciplined and who is not by the way they act and how they go about their day.

We will go over a list of these traits, so you have a good idea of what to expect while you are in the beginning stages of being more disciplined yourself. Once you start adopting these traits, it will show. You won't have to say a single word to declare that you are self-disciplined. These are the traits that you'll likely develop over time:

Resisting temptation: Obviously, temptation is the enemy of discipline. No matter how hard you want to give into it, you know that within yourself is the power to control yourself. Temptation can be powerful only if you allow it to happen. Temptation comes at the worst times (like emotional low points). As long as you are aware of its presence and decide not to give in, you're in the driver's seat.

Endless commitment: Those who are disciplined and committed speak their words and stick to it. When they declare a goal that they want to accomplish, they stick with it. Period. End of story. When you say it to other people, some of them may keep a watchful eye on you. So, when they ask you how it's going, how will you respond? With shock and aghast? Or with confidence knowing that you got it done.

They take good care of themselves: A person who takes care of themselves is not only disciplined, but they also have a high level of self-respect that can't be matched. They take care of themselves mentally and physically and do it with a plan in place every day.

They set limits and boundaries: A disciplined person knows their limits and their boundaries. They set them and never go beyond them. In other words, they say no to things easily. They don't want to cross a line they set for themselves. Limits and boundaries are a true test for discipline. Keep within them and you will certainly pass.

Emotions are second to them: When it comes to taking action, their emotions take a backseat (and rightfully so). Whenever there is a goal or a task that needs to be done, they do it anyways even if they don't feel like doing it. The task of overriding your emotions and performing a routine task can be difficult for most people. Thus, doing so will lead to procrastination.

They set a deadline and meet it: You have a goal to achieve and want to meet it in six months. No "pushing it back". No "rescheduling". No nothing. They stick with the deadline and keep at it until that day (or before that). Is it fine to complete the task ahead of schedule? You bet. You must resist the urge to procrastinate or wait for a time where motivation appears to get the tasks done.

The prize is the focus: There are plenty of words that you can conjure up in the English language that will be a nugget of truth. "Keep your eye on the prize" is one of them. Whether you have a setback or two or fell off the wagon and haven't gotten anything done in days, knowing what the end reward is and focusing on it is key.

You will soon remember that you have a goal to accomplish and you'll do whatever it takes to get it done regardless of what's getting in the way.

They focus on the small things: When it comes to achieving a bigger goal, they know that it comes down to focus on the small things. They break up the much larger goal into little pieces. Think of it like a music album. You can't just record one song and call it good. You can record ten of them and have a hit album that your fans will love. One song equals a step towards achieving your much larger goal. The same can be said about a book. Write a thousand words and you are closer to getting the entire thing done. Get the idea?

MAKE FRIENDS WITH PEOPLE WHO ARE SMARTER THAN YOU

There's an old saying: "If you are the smartest person in the room, find another room where you are not". Not only will this help you build more discipline and mental toughness, it will humble you in the fact that there may be someone who is more disciplined than you, smarter than you, and has accomplished more. Don't let this be a personal indictment against you. These people are not your enemies. They are people you can learn from and inspire you to be your best self.

Now, the question is: how will you surround yourself with people smarter than you? Supplementally, where exactly can you find them? The answer may seem like something you might not expect, but people who are smarter than you can be found just about anywhere. It's a matter of knowing how to spot them.

SIGNS THAT SOMEONE IS SMARTER THAN YOU

It's not that there is a specific place where you can find people smarter than you (aside from maybe a local MENSA chapter meeting). Being observant is key when seeking out people who are smarter than you. We'll be taking a look at the following six signs that will help you determine whether or not that person is smarter than you. One caveat though: they may exhibit one sign and be completely dumb. So, it's important to look for at least two or three signs before making a confirmation.

Here's what you should look for:

They talk less, listen more: This seems like a no brainer thing to do. Most people got smart just by listening to people and speaking at the right opportunities. They can ask questions to gain more information or seek clarification on a statement they're trying to understand.

They specialize in something: A smart person is usually a specialist in one area. Sure, they have interests in broad topics. But there's always that one thing they will talk about for twenty minutes straight and never get tired of doing. They know the ins and outs. They know things about their specialty that most people don't.

Excellent management skills: When a smart person is a leader or a manager, they don't want to be the only smart person in the group. They want their subordinates to gain knowledge and will waste no time spreading that wealth of knowledge with other people. As long as they find people who are willing to learn, it might seem simple enough to do.

Pressing on when things go south: This goes without saying. But smart people are usually disciplined and mentally tough. One such example that proves this is their ability to handle things that don't go in their favor with as little stress as possible. They laugh off simple mistakes and move on instead of dwelling on them. Also, when things go wrong, they always have a few alternative plans up their sleeves. They're like magicians in a sense. What the conflict sees, they are being fooled by the smart person who has already "escaped" with an alternative solution.

They use social media, but not in the usual way: At some point, a smart person will rely on social media as a source of information. They won't engage in any of the petty, toxic stuff that most people will use social media for. They might be on social media for the purpose of communicating with family and close friends. Other than that, a smart person doesn't care much for it.

They don't make people look stupid: A smart person will never make someone look stupid. It would be easy to do, yet there's a caveat. If they try to make a person look bad, that will boomerang back to them and they themselves will look bad as well. Talk about a counterintuitive task. Instead, they try to make them into a smart person.

Now that you know these signs, you will have a less difficult time trying to spot the smartest people you can find. You can come across them by complete accident just by having random conversations with them. Also, getting connected with smart people and building a network will take time and effort. But it will be nice to have on hand knowing you have a question to ask or need to seek some kind of advice.

In this day in age, you can follow people who are smarter than you on social media. Find out what they are reading or sharing. Find ways to connect with them. If they fit your ideal profile of who you want to connect with, then add them to a list of people who you want to meet. These don't have to be big name people at first. If you shoot for the big-name people first, it will be very difficult to connect with them since there are plenty of gatekeepers (not to mention, their busy schedules will be a pain to navigate).

TIPS ON WHAT SMART PEOPLE DO

If you want to become smart and actually know the part, it's important to know what they do (other than the traits listed above). Here are some things that we suggest:

Read: That's what you're doing now, right? Plus, there are other books that you might want to consider reading as well. So long as they are of interest to you, have at it. One more thing, what topic are you interested in gaining knowledge in? Once you have an idea, start by reading some of the best books (along with some related titles).

Dress the part: This may sound a bit ridiculous. But there's usually a pattern of how smart people dress. Usually they are well-dressed, well-groomed, and take good care of themselves. If you follow people who are smarter than you, observe how they are dressed. This doesn't mean you have to wear a suit and tie all the time. But something that makes you look presentable.

Communicate effectively: What's the difference between someone who rushes while they talk and someone who talks slowly, articulately, and pauses at the right moments? One of them is an effective communicator. The person who talks like they are in a hurry don't communicate effectively. And they will often stumble all over the place. Someone who talks slow, gets to the point, and pauses to gather their thoughts before continuing will be perceived as much smarter.

Learn to easily build rapport: When connecting with people who you want to include in your network, building rapport is key. Get to know them a bit. Try not to reach for anything too personal early on in the interaction.

There are plenty of things smart people can do (and so will you with practice). Smart people do things a certain way subconsciously. They weren't born to communicate effectively or have an easy time to build rapport. They've learned it. Smart people know how to build themselves into better versions of themselves.

TAKE THE PROACTIVE APPROACH

A disciplined and smart person is always looking for the proactive approach instead of the reactive. When you are proactive, you are taking responsibility. Those who are proactive don't place blame on other people or things that are within control. Sounds familiar, doesn't it? Reactive people do the exact opposite of what we've just mentioned. Show us someone who is disciplined and reactive and we'll show you someone that has never told a lie in their lifetime.

So, what is the difference between being proactive and reactive? Let's take a look at the following scenario: For example, if some kid called you stupid for no apparent reason, what would you do? A reactive person would justify that they are not stupid and maybe even hassle the kid. A proactive person meanwhile will have that choice to react that way or ignore it and move on. In their heads, they don't care about some bratty kid's opinion. They will usually do the same thing if someone who is an adult called someone stupid for no reason.

The one true difference between a proactive and a reactive person is choice. A reactive person has already chosen to react while a proactive person has a different avenue to travel. It seems like a simple thing to do, but many people don't know nor practice this.

Reactive people will let things that are beyond their control get to them. A proactive person will understand that these exist and there is nothing that they can do. But they know of some alternatives and workarounds. For example, if you're a mom or dad who is planning on taking your son out for a picnic at the park and it rains, you can take him to lunch at your favorite restaurant instead. No big deal, there's always an alternative.

A reactive person will feel bad about not being able to do something with their kids and will feel like they've failed as a parent (when in reality, it's not their fault). Things beyond your control will either influence your behavior or allow you to act accordingly based on alternative plans that you might have laid out in advance (or thought of on the spot).

RECAP

When it comes to discipline, it should be treated as if it were your own child. You want to birth it and nurture it. The last thing you want to do is harm it by making mistakes that seem like harmless tasks (like procrastination). Another thing you shouldn't worry about is finding motivation. Forget the fact that such a thing exists. Just do the task anyways even if you don't feel like doing it. You'll have a sense of accomplishment and know that having a crappy day isn't going to stop you from completing the day's tasks.

Someone who lives a disciplined life possesses traits that can be easily acquired. They are committed to sticking to their goals, placing their emotions in the back seat, and keeping their eye on the prize no matter what. They will do their best to conquer their goals and get the job done no matter what life throws at them.

If you want to learn more about living a more disciplined life, it's best to go to the source: the smartest people you know. They are usually more disciplined and mentally tougher than most. Do your best to connect with them be it online or in person. These will be people you can learn from or even form lifelong friendships with.

Finally, taking the proactive approach instead of a reactive approach will definitely be a boost for your discipline and mental toughness. It will challenge you to handle things beyond your control in a more appropriate manner. You'll learn how to come up with alternative plans when things don't go your way. And you'll learn that it's pointless to blame other people or things on the negative things affecting your life.

A proactive person is smart, sees some good in the bad, and will always come out on top in the end. It's a matter of how they choose to react in a negative situation.

6

REACHING FOR YOUR HIGHEST GOALS AND AIMING FOR TRUE FREEDOM

E veryone has a goal that is the highest of them all. And for most, achieving it may seem next to impossible. However, as long as they have the right mindset, they can achieve it. In this chapter, we'll be talking about setting those goals, attaining them, and being able to live a life of true freedom.

We'll talk about the things that might move you in the right direction? What will be enough for you to get started and stay in a forward direction. Before you know it, you'll be able to move in the right direction without having any problems. Even with slight setbacks, you'll know exactly what to do and where to go.

This chapter will show you exactly what it takes to reach your goals. You'll learn that there are many ways to set goals and attain them. But for the sake of simplicity, we'll show you one way to approach them with ease. If you want to achieve your goals and easily do so without procrastination, keep reading.

WHAT MOVES YOU?

What is something that moves you? What gets you out of bed in the morning? These are just a couple of questions worth asking. There's always something that you love doing to a point where you get never tired of it. It's the one thing that will turn you from being lazy to a person of action.

Another thing that can move you is influence. However, there are three types of influence that exist: negative, neutral, and positive. Let's face it: influence and control are something we want in our lives. And that's one of the few reasons why you're reading this book right now. You want total control over most things in your life. You want to be free from the entities that tie you down and limit what control you have at the moment.

We also want to set an example for those who seek our influence. The last thing we want to be are bad influences on others. Speaking of seeking influence, you're more likely looking for it yourself. The only kind of influence you want to see are those who are on the positive side. Needless to say, there are positive influences that are watching your every move (and you might not even know it). Who exactly are these positive influences? Your parents, your spouse, your children, anyone who plays a positive and important role in your life.

Naturally, these are the people who will be your best friends and cheerleaders. If you are a parent, your children are watching you. If anything, you are responsible for being the influential figure in their life. So, it would be best for you to set the best example for them possible, so they learn from you.

Whether you know it or not, your actions no matter how big or small will play an influential role. You can influence someone in your life without saying a word. Avoid bad influences as much as you can. Their actions (or inactions) might just draw you in and you may mimic what they're doing. This is something you don't want to do when your ultimate goal is to be your most disciplined and be mentally tough.

WHO ARE YOUR LIFE-CHANGING INFLUENCERS?

Jesus Christ. Mother Teresa. Abraham Lincoln. Elon Musk.

These are just a few names of people that may earn the title of life changing influencers. These historical figures and big names may have a set of words and actions that can impact people in such a positive way. But do your life-changing influencers have to be famous people? Absolutely not. They can be members of your family you have never met in your life.

The truth is, there are a couple people you'll come across in your life who will who will change your life for the better. You will be fortunate to learn from them, admire them, and talk highly about them long after they pass away. Who knows? You could be that life-changing influencer in someone's life. You could be living or dead and still make some kind of impact on a person.

Take a moment to think about your ideal life-changing influencers. Who do you aspire to be more like? What is it about them that draws you to them? Why do you consider them influencers? These are just a few questions that you should consider asking yourself.

There's bound to be one in your life even at this point in your life. Who was one of your favorite teachers in school? Do you consider them to be a disciplined and mentally tough individual? What was it about their classes that drew you to take them? Remember, there is plenty of room for you to include another influencer in your life that will change you for the better.

MOVING AS IF EVERYTHING IS EFFORTLESS

Do you ever watch shows like "American Ninja Warrior" or "Titan"? These are TV shows where people with insane athletic abilities show-case their talents by going through obstacle courses in a timely manner. These are not your usual obstacle courses like running around cones or alternating between feet on a tire course.

These competitors cross through rickety bridges, rappel up walls, and walk through balance beams quickly. If you fall into the mud or water, you lose. To the average person, it seems like a very difficult task to do. But for the contestants of these shows, they have put in plenty of work to make sure they are in top physical condition.

When practicing for these competitions, they practice without making any kind of effort. They also perform tasks that may sound impossible for the average person to do (as if it were almost uncharacteristic of them). They train hard, change their diets to accommodate said training, and put in the work even on days when they don't want to. On top of that, they make sacrifices in order to focus more on their training. The lesson here is they had a system in place where they were able to achieve their goals. Their ultimate goal was to compete in "American Ninja Warrior" or "Titan".

They know that winning it all would be the cherry on top. But just being on there is just enough for them. After all that hard work and dedication, they've made it.

Getting to the point: the lesson is that they have put in the practice and the work to make everything effortless. They are aware of the mistakes they make and how many times they will happen. They don't complain or think that they suck at what they do. They get back up, plow through it, and get it done.

What causes effortless achievement to be "impossible"?

For most of us, our desire to get moving without little to no motivation is what we look for. How great would it be for us to get out of bed in the morning and do something without effort or fail? Unfortunately, that seems to be within a much farther reach. It seems like whenever we want to do something, we don't feel like it and would rather be lazy all day.

Achieving our goals with little to no effort is possible. But how do we get there? The key to go from wanting to do something to doing it anyway can be summed up into these words: emotional understanding. How do you approach emotional understanding?

How this works is you take a look at the goal you want to achieve. From there, you will be able to examine why it's so difficult to achieve it. What makes it so unpleasant? Once you have a good idea of why it seems like such a monumental task to achieve, only then you can disconnect the negative associations from it. Specifically, the negative emotions and associations of doing a goal are usually the "I don't want to do it" or "I don't feel like doing it". Some will even use the excuse of the work being "too hard". That's a sign of emotional resistance. And that's just another sign of letting your emotions control you instead of the other way around.

What you need to do is learn what your emotional blockers are? If your goal is to climb Denali in Alaska, but you're afraid of heights then your fear of heights is an emotional blocker. There are three types of emotional blockers that exist:

Immediate: This kind of emotional blocker stems from what you actually dislike about achieving the goal itself. In other words, what is it about the goal you want to achieve that you hate? Is it something you hate having to do? You need to perform the task anyways no matter how much you're going to hate it. A real-life example of this is not being able to spend time with your family because of an important deadline coming up. While you are not ignoring them in the slightest, you need a lot of time and attention to accomplish a goal that will mean big things for your business. You hate having to sacrifice that time that would otherwise be spent on those you love. But without that sacrifice, you and your family won't be better off.

Identity: This comes down to negative self-talk. "You can't get it done because you're terrible at X." You say to yourself that you're not the type of person to achieve a goal you plan on setting. You can be your own self. But you can be a better version if you achieve the goals you set, even if it's uncharacteristic of you. There's nothing more satisfying than someone telling you that there is something different about you (and in a good way).

Receiving: These are basically certain beliefs that you adopt that are preventing you from the goal you want to achieve. For example, someone may be struggling to achieve a certain task but have too much pride to ask for help. They don't want to be perceived as weak. We're all human. And when humans struggle, they are not afraid to ask for help.

You should take a moment and think about the kind of emotional blockers you have dealt with in the past. It doesn't have to be too long of a list. Think of five different emotional blockers you have dealt with in the past. Think of the goals you want to accomplish and look ahead. What kind of immediate blockers do you see? What are you willing to sacrifice for the sake of reaching your goal (but would find hard to give up)?

What kind of negative self-talk have you given yourself? And lastly, what are the emotional blockers that happen as you move closer to achieving your goal? Are you too proud to ask for help? Are you saying to yourself that such a goal is impossible?

Being able to assess what your emotional blockers are and being able to conquer them will help you become more able to attain your goals without the effort and motivation needed.

ADDITIONAL TIPS FOR EFFORTLESSLY ACHIEVING YOUR GOALS

As you venture towards your journey in achieving your highest goals, you'll want to take the following seven tips below. It's understandable that there are things you don't want to do. At the same time, your negative emotions are mostly to blame for your inaction or slow moving towards the goals you set.

Here are some things to take into consideration:

Delegate it, if need be: Don't know how to do a certain task? Do you know how but don't have the time? Delegate it to someone who will get it done for you. We can't juggle everything all at once. As humans, we have our limits. There are times when a goal that needs to be achieved where it will take more than one person to accomplish it. Delegate to someone who has the skill and competence and you'll feel a lot better.

Eliminate the old goals: You probably have a to do list that has goals that you have never gotten around to or tried to achieve (but never materialized). The only thing to do at this point is eliminate them all together. What's the point in trying to get them done when it's going to sit there and collect dust? Instead, focus on goals that interest you and make you happy.

Know your boundaries: In the previous chapter, we've talked about setting boundaries. It's important to remind yourself what they are and what you need to do to stay within them.

Eliminate distractions: We've already covered distractions earlier on in the book. By now, you should have a basic idea on how to eliminate both external and internal distractions. If not, refer to Chapter 3 on how you can minimize them to your advantage.

Find the right tools for the job: Depending on the goals you want to achieve, it's important to find the right tools that will work. If you are using something that is not working effectively then it would be time to find something that is new, much more functional, and able to get the job done.

Change what isn't working: If you are doing something that isn't working, what's the point in doing the same thing over and over again expecting a different result (which is insanity, of course). Change it up and see if it works. If it does, good. If not, repeat the process until something is working.

Double down on what's working: If you know what is working in terms of achieving your goals, this is a good opportunity to double down on it. If you are putting in the work, you can put in double the work if you are up to the challenge. The more you double down, the faster you can achieve your highest goal without half-assing it or reducing the quality of it.

3 IS A MANAGEABLE NUMBER TO START WORKING ON

Whoever coined the term "it's easy as 1, 2, 3" obviously hit the nail on the head. When you start setting goals that you want to achieve, you want the process to be as simple as possible. Step one, step two, step three, done. Sounds kind of nice, right? In this brief section, we'll show you a three-step newbie-friendly way to set the goals you want to achieve. Later on in the chapter, we'll talk about the different methods of goal setting that you can use.

Now, here is the three-step process to help you set your goals so you can achieve them with ease:

1. **Set three manageable goals:** Seems simple enough, right? Three simple goals that you can easily attain in a short amount of time would be a good start. Five goals would be pushing it. Ten might be torture (especially if you are starting out).

2. **Make sure they are high, but attainable:** You want the goals to be a bit of a challenge. But nothing too difficult. You want them to stretch a bit. If you don't, they will likely be considered "to-do" items and not goals.

3. **Put together a series of "To-Dos" in one list:** You can set "to-do" tasks into a list that can form that goal you want to achieve. The best technique for something like this is the SMART technique (which we will learn in the next section).

THERE ARE MULTIPLE WAYS TO SET YOUR GOALS, BUT YOU SHOULD CHOOSE ONE THAT WORKS BEST FOR YOU

In this section, we'll be talking about three goal management methods that will work to your advantage. They include the following:

SMART, HARD, and WOOP. You're probably wondering "what the heck are they"? We'll break down each method so you have a better understanding of what they are and how you can use them. First, let's break down SMART:

THE SMART METHOD

Wasting no time, let's take a look at SMART:

Specific: What is the specific goal that you want to achieve? Rather than be vague about it like say "make more money" you can say "Make $10,000 by December 31st by starting a content marketing agency for eCommerce stores". Or instead of "lose weight", you can say you want to "lose 10 pounds in six weeks by working out three times a week for 15 minutes". The more specific you whittle it down to, the better.

Measurable: You obviously need to keep track of your goals. And one of the best ways to do it is measure them. You won't be able to know how far you've gotten if you don't have the metrics or the data. Without them, you won't be able to determine whether or not making a change towards achieving your goal is possible.

Attainable: If your goal is realistic, it can be attainable. How long can you achieve the goal itself? Don't set lofty goals and think you can achieve it in the quickest amount of time possible. If you want to earn $10,000 (for example), think of a realistic time frame. Can you do it in six months? Possible, but it will be difficult. How about a year? Sounds realistic enough.

Relevant: Is this goal relative to your values? Is this the kind of goal that will make you happy? Does it fall in line with your personal beliefs? These are some of the questions you need to ask yourself to ensure that your goals are relevant to you.

Time-bound: It's always a good idea to set a timeframe to when the goal can be achieved. You can't say you want to do X and Y without a specific time frame. Again, think realistically here. For smaller goals, set a shorter time frame. For example, if you want to lose five pounds, six weeks might be a good time frame. If you want to lose 20 pounds, consider three months might be good enough.

THE HARD TECHNIQUE

Next, we'll be taking a look at the HARD technique. Here's what HARD stands for:

Heartfelt: Sometimes, investing your emotions towards your goals may be necessary. Why do you care about this goal? What is your emotional attachment? Is it because of someone you love? What's that one emotion that's driving you to achieve that goal?

Animated: This will help you think ahead to what will occur after the fact. Visualize yourself in a scene where you have just achieved the goal of your dreams. How do you feel? What kind of emotions are you sensing?

Required: What are the concrete reasons that are helping you achieve those goals? What has to get done? What goals need to be done urgently?

Difficulty: This is where you really want to challenge yourself. You intentionally want to make the goal difficult so you can face the challenges head on. Although, we stress that you shouldn't make it harder than it has to be. Set some challenges that can be difficult to accomplish. But be aware of the challenge ahead so you can prepare yourself to conquer it at every opportunity.

THE WOOP TECHNIQUE

Lastly, we'll take a look at the WOOP Technique: This is perfect for when you want to break old habits and form new ones. Let's get right to it:

Wish: What goal are you excited about achieving? What is it that you dream about? Think of what it is and be sure that it is a realistic enough goal to achieve.

Outcome: What is the outcome that you want to achieve? Picture it in your mind.

Obstacle: What obstacles will stand in the way of this goal? Being aware of them before you even move forward will put you at a greater advantage of going up against them. You can navigate the obstacles with ease and simplicity. You'll know about what could hold you back. At the same time, you'll need to form a battle plan to attack the obstacles and move forward.

Plan: Without a plan, you do nothing. Plan the initial steps you need to take. Plan some alternatives in case you hit some dead-ends or obstacles. Planning ahead of time will put you at an even greater advantage.

One of these techniques can work to your advantage. It's important to test one out and see which one will be more effective. As mentioned before, the WOOP technique is perfect for anyone looking to form a new habit while kicking old ones to the curb. If you are looking to start a new online business and plan on growing it over time, the SMART technique might be better suited for such a thing.

DEFINE YOUR FREEDOM AND BE ACCOUNTABLE

True freedom is worth accomplishing. You want to break free from the prison that is your mind of a negative mindset. The late Sean Stephenson once said that your mind is like a prison. You can escape it at any time since there is no guard or barb wire fence. But what keeps you inside that prison is your limiting self-belief.

The truth is, you can acquire true freedom just by busting out of that prison. From there, you are free to move in any direction. So long as it takes you to your ultimate destination (your main goal). Freedom is possible, but the only obstacle standing in our way is ourselves.

Freedom is different from one person to the other. One person wants to be free in spirit. The other wants to attain freedom in the sense of not being tied down by their financial issues. Freedom is not some kind of political term. It's something that can be acquired in a physical, spiritual, and psychological sense. You can physically free yourself from a life of potential health issues by losing weight. You can be free from psychological setbacks and mental blocks if you decide to push forward and change your mindset for the better.

The one thing you need to know about acquiring freedom is having awareness. You must be aware that you aren't completely free until you've taken the steps to achieve it. Once you are aware of your newfound freedom, the mission is accomplished. Awareness is the first and last step.

In this instance, you are aware that you are not in the right mindset. You are not in a state where you are disciplined or mentally tough to handle life's challenges. Prison is hell (literally and figuratively). In this context, living a life where discipline and mental toughness does not exist might be your own personal hell. You can break free from comfort and complacency. You can escape negativity with the right kind of escape plan that is being outlined in this book.

Jocko Wilinik said it best: discipline equals freedom. To translate it in plain English, as long as you have control you will have freedom. Control over your mindset, your daily habits, and everything in between. If you accept discipline, you earn freedom. Jocko is disciplined enough to get up every morning at 4:30 AM, allowing him more time in the day. You don't have to get up early in the morning to attain this.

If you want financial freedom, you must instill financial discipline. Stop spending your money on needless things. You can save money and have it ready in a moment's notice when some not so pleasant financial situation rears its ugly head. You will have the freedom to get rid of it quickly before the problem gets worse. Holding yourself accountable and making sure that you make intelligent financial decisions will ensure that you keep up with your usual expenses, so you don't find yourself in a jeopardizing situation (such as eviction from your home).

HOW TO HOLD YOURSELF ACCOUNTABLE

Holding yourself accountable is one of the key skills to have in order to achieve true freedom. Failure to do so will lessen your chances. Here are some tips that you should follow in order to hold yourself more accountable now and in the future:

Don't reveal your goals: One of the most fatal mistakes anyone can make is revealing their goals and intentions to anyone. The more they disclose, the more pressure you'll put on yourself (especially when people ask you how things are going). Remember, you never know who is watching you actually attain that specific goal you set forth. Contrary to popular belief, announcing your goals is not the best way to hold yourself accountable. People want premature praise for an accomplishment that may never materialize. Not only that, you may receive negative feedback before you even move forward with your goal. And that alone could mentally paralyze someone and thus they never start in the first place.

Write down your goals: If you have a goal that you want to achieve, put it to paper. Better yet, start with a major goal and put together a simple list on how you want to achieve it. These include your short-term and long-term goals. Make sure you have it written nice and neat on a piece of paper or notebook.

Put together a mission statement: A mission statement defines who you are, the goals you want to achieve, and the values you hold dear. No need for it to be long like a novel. Keep it short, sweet, and to the point.

Review your overall performance: Taking a look at how you performed overall will give you a view at what you've done right, what you've done wrong, and what you can do to improve at the next opportunity.

Don't be afraid to ask for feedback: Feedback is important. Ask your fellow team members or your support network. You will get positive feedback. But not all of it will be positive at all. Use the negative feedback as an opportunity to make some changes and adjustments where necessary.

SELF-DISCIPLINE CAN CREATE MORE FREEDOM THAN EVER BEFORE IN YOUR LIFE

This can't be stressed enough. Being able to discipline yourself will help you create the kind of freedom that you want. Self-discipline allows you to gain control and therefore gives you the freedom to do whatever you want. Freedom allows you flexibility, indulgence, and allowance. So, the two go hand in hand.

Simply put, discipline is the giver of freedom. It is never a taker. That is why it is important to put yourself first to an extent. But in some situations, putting yourself last is equally as important. If you are a parent, you always put your family first. It's all about making the right decision that will benefit not just you but the most important people in your life.

Self-discipline will force you to make decisions that may be hard, but in the end, they were good decisions. For example, if you are trying to live a healthy lifestyle, it may seem tough to give up the fast food. But instead of going for that number one with a Coke, you opt for a salad and a bottle of water instead. It's hard to let go of the things you are used to. But in the end, it's worth it. Learn to embrace these kinds of decisions and you'll make them without breaking a sweat.

The question for you is simply this: how far are you willing to go to attain self-discipline? What are you willing to give up? What are you most passionate about focusing on? The reward of freedom is sweet when you are consistent with self-discipline.

INDULGE IN YOUR GREATEST PLEASURE AND HOBBIES 'GUILT FREE' AND WITHOUT ANY FORM OF PROCRASTINATION

When you are self-disciplined, you will be able to do more instead of less. You will get to enjoy doing the things that you love. The goals that you want to achieve are easy to attain. You can be able to work on that passion project that you've been putting off for so long. You will feel no shame. And you will not feel the need to procrastinate.

It's important to let in what you want to bring into your life and let out what you want to get rid of. It's hard to let go of the things you've once enjoyed. But once you realize it was more of a waste of time than a true return on investment, you'll realize that letting it go won't be so bad after all.

RECAP

Being able to reach for your highest goals and attaining true freedom in the process is possible. It all boils down to being disciplined enough to get it done. As someone who is on the path towards discipline and mental toughness, you realize that you are setting an example for those keeping a close eye on you. You will develop into a positive influence for someone important in your life. Plus, you also model yourself after the people in your life who are considered life changing influencers.

Being able to move towards your goal without a lot of effort will come down to one thing: being able to be consistent and put in the work. Don't worry about making mistakes or the setbacks that happen. As long as you are aware of those setbacks, you'll be ready for them whether they pop up or not. Think of yourself as someone who is competing for American Ninja Warrior. Your goal that you want to attain is at the other end of the course.

When managing your goals, it's as easy as 1,2,3 in planning them. However, you'll want to consider a method to set your goals. Whether you want to be SMART about it or WOOP it up, there's a method that will work for just about anyone.

Your freedom is your reward for being self-disciplined and holding yourself accountable. This will allow you to give yourself more time to work on a passion project, more financial freedom and the ability to knock out any financial problems before they worsen, and the freedom to do whatever you feel like doing. The freedom to do something is possible to attain so long as you are willing to discipline yourself.

IV

LEARN TO LOVE THE
PROCESS, YOU CAN'T SKIP IT

7

DEVELOPING DISCIPLINE

This chapter will cover step by step on how you should develop discipline. If anything, it should be built block by block. It should be like a brick wall or a tall building. The higher it goes, the higher your level of discipline is. Discipline will help you focus on the tasks that you want to get done while allowing you to develop the ability to restrain yourself from veering off course.

We'll talk about whether or not motivation is enough or not. We'll also talk about what discipline should not be used for. The power of discipline is useful in many situations. But there are times when it may not be needed. We'll also talk about how to handle your urges and how you should simply "ride the wave" instead of being swallowed by it.

This chapter will show you how to make the easy and hard choices without breaking a sweat. The decision making we face on a regular basis can be as simple as ordering a pizza or as difficult as crossing a high wire. Even making the toughest decisions possible may seem effortless (even in situations where either decision will yield some kind of negative consequence).

Lastly, you will learn the kind of self-discipline developed by professional athletes and Navy SEALs. These are the type of people who face monumental tasks on a regular basis. And they do the hard things without fail or little effort needed. This chapter is something you really want to pay attention to. Especially when you want to develop discipline. Let's begin:

MOTIVATION IS GOOD AND ALL, BUT IT IS NOT ENOUGH

Early in the book, we stated that motivation is something that is elusive if you search for it. We also said that you don't need to find motivation to start on a task. Do it anyways even if you don't feel like it. Motivation is like a cat. It comes to you at times when you least expect it.

Even if motivation finds you, it won't be enough. However, there are some links to the chain that you want to add. We'll be talking about aspiration and dedication. Both of these are what you need aside from motivation itself to achieve the tasks that are set forth. Putting the three together will mix into the perfect blend of discipline.

Let's discuss each of these things starting with aspiration:

The Importance of Aspiration

Aspiration is defined as the ambition or hope of achieving a specific goal or task. In a team setting, the goals and targets that you as a team set forth can be accomplished with ease if they are aligned within your aspirations. When that happens, the engagement levels will increase. The team will work together as one giant unit.

Before the team works together, they need to know what's in it for them. What exactly will be the end goal for the team? How will they be rewarded for a job well done? If there is nothing they get in return, what's the point in working together?

When a team knows that there is a reward at the end of the tunnel, the team will work together. So long as there are no personal differences that will affect the team's morale or the like, the team can accomplish the goal in front of them. One of our basic needs that need to be met according to the Maslow Hierarchy is the sense of achievement and recognition for what we do. It doesn't matter if you work as part of a team or achieve something in terms of individual efforts. There is no better feeling like accomplishing something of value and being recognized for it. The problem is most people decide to let it go unnoticed.

Aspiration is one of the key things that you need in order to be disciplined. What is your biggest aspiration? How will you achieve it? What obstacles will likely stand in the way of it? And what will you do to conquer those obstacles and move forward?

Why is dedication equally important?

Dedication and motivation are not the same. Dedication is making a decision and honoring it at every possible opportunity. You are committed to starting the goal or task and seeing it through to the end. It is dedication that separates those who are the true winners from those who just quit when things go south.

Dedication is what happens when motivation is nowhere to be found, but you do the work anyways. Because the sooner you complete a task or get closer to your goal, the better you'll feel knowing you've made the right decision. When things go wrong, you don't give up. When you fall off the horse, you get back up and ride again. That is what dedication is all about.

When you or your team is faced with setbacks, it's important to assess what they are and handle them accordingly. After that, you keep pressing forward. You don't stop, drop everything, and call it good. When the job is half done, it's not good enough. There will be those on the team that may quit on you halfway through. Either you carry on and let someone take on a bit of an extra load. Or find someone who is competent and positive enough to take on the challenges that still lie ahead for the team.

Dedication is one thing that no living individual can ever ignore or exclude from recognizing someone's achievements.

DISCIPLINE SHOULD NOT BE USED FOR ACTIVITIES & TASKS LIKE THIS...

One of the things where discipline should not be used is when you are doing creative activities. Creativity is more of a process instead of a discipline. Discipline teaches you to keep within your boundaries and limits. With creativity, there are a set of rules that can be followed. However, you can break them as you please. They mostly won't care for limitations and will likely branch off on different paths in search of new discoveries. You often see this with artists and musicians. They hate being able to keep within the normal boundaries and rules. So, they dare to walk a tight line and create something that takes things a step further.

You can use discipline when doing creative things. But at the same time, you don't have to be a follower of any rules. It sounds like a paradox because discipline and rules seem to go hand in hand. Discipline and creativity shall never meet. Any creative project will seem like a job if you incorporate discipline. Creativity in one aspect is like discipline: it gives you freedom. In this context, you have the freedom to let your creativity run wild. When the inspiration hits you, you add something to what you're currently creating or start from scratch. Either way, the rules won't apply, and discipline is not necessary in this regard.

RIDING THE WAVE OF YOUR URGES

In this section, we're going to talk about "urge surfing". What is it exactly? It's basically addressing impulsive behaviors. Specifically, they are mostly associated with addictions such as binge eating or drinking large amounts of alcohol on a regular basis. When you feel the need to have a drink or eat a lot to deal with a negative emotion, it's easy just to give in and get it done.

But with urge surfing, it's an entirely different thing. This is a mindfulness technique that you can use to your advantage each time you have an urge. You don't act on that addictive behavior. Instead, you meditate and let it pass through you. This is a lot better than trying to fight it.

How do you do this mindfulness technique? First off, close your eyes. Imagine that you are riding on a surfboard. That giant wave you are riding is your urge. Imagine riding the ups and downs of that wave. You are closing in on the shoreline that will guide you towards freedom and discipline. Typically, an urge will last 20 to 30 minutes.

Any pro surfer can tell you that you can ride the wave with ease, or you can make one wrong move and the wave comes crashing down on you. With urge surfing, whatever you don't do will get weaker (and whatever you do will get stronger). The more you act on your urge, the stronger it gets (and vice versa).

Urge surfing for best results

This urge surfing technique will allow you to meditate for intervals of one to five minutes. After each interval, you should reassess your urge. If you are still feeling it, repeat the process. You'll start to notice that urge subsiding little by little as you go. Doing this repeatedly will help you break that connection between you and the urge itself.

Alternatives to consider

Even though riding the urge wave is one thing to handle it, you should also consider other alternatives in order for it to pass. For example, you can talk to a friend or family member for a while. Or you can watch something educational on YouTube. Do something that will help you get your mind off of the urge and focused on something else.

The easier you are able to do this, the better you'll be able to handle any urge no matter how sudden it appears. You can perform these tasks in between meditation sessions if you wish. From time to time, you should check to see if the urge is still existent.

Urge surfing is the perfect way for you to gain control over your urges. You can literally suck the power right out of your urges and beat them into submission with ease once you get the hang of it.

MAKING YOUR CHOICE, EITHER IT'S EASY OR HARD

We face countless decisions every single day. Most of them are usually easy. Some of them may be hard. But in the end, it's you that determines whether or not that decision is either or. You can make it easy on yourself or harder than it has to be. It's true that there are some decisions you make that will be tough because of the ramifications that follow. For example, a manager may be faced with the task of letting go of one employee due to cutbacks. The company is hemorrhaging money, and someone may need to be let go just to save money.

Sometimes, the hard decisions can yield some positive results no matter how unpopular it is in the eyes of other people. In terms of growth and discipline, making the decisions you hate is a likely thing to happen.

HOW TO MAKE BETTER DECISIONS

Having the ability to make better decisions even under pressure will put you at a greater advantage compared to others. We'll be taking a look at the following tips below, so you'll be able to make better decisions. Even high-pressure decisions can be made with little effort as possible. Let's take a look at these tips:

1. **Always go with your gut:** This should be rule number one in anyone's decision making rule book. You'd be crazy to go against your gut. It will never steer you wrong 99 percent of the time. Your gut will be able to tell you what's right and what's wrong before your consciousness even gets to it. Unconscious decision making can save your hide in the most high-pressure situations. If you get that "funny" feeling when faced with a potential life-altering decision, then you'll want to address it. Don't even dare to ignore it.

2. **You don't always have to ask everyone:** It's admirable to ask people for their opinion on something before making a decision. However, if it's a high-pressure decision you'll face more problems when you hear two different opinions. One person tells you to do it and the other tells you not to. And that's where the pressure gets cranked up to another

level. Sometimes, it's better to never seek the opinion of others at all.

3. **Ask yourself the right questions:** How will this decision benefit me and the others? What will be the outcome if I make decision A? What about decision B? These are questions you'll want to ask yourself. It's good to carefully weigh the pros and cons of each decision. Sometimes, either decision is a lose-lose. It's a matter of what kind of repercussions will deal a lesser blow once the decision itself is made.

4. **Consider your values:** It's easy to make a decision so long as it aligns with your values. However, there may be decisions where neither of them will be on par with them. It's important to know what your core values are and how they define your life. Write down a list of your highest values. Make sure that it is clear and easy to understand. That way, whenever you need to fall back on them for references, you'll have a good idea of what you believe in. Especially when it comes to making the right kind of decisions.

5. **Be aware of the effects:** Each decision has an effect that will alter the course of future events. Imagine that you're about to give a presentation to investors for the purpose of getting more capital for your business. But there is one problem: you have a fear of public speaking. If you back out now because of your fears, you'll never get the capital you need, and your business will suffer. Press on and get through it, you can impress them enough to get the money. Even if

the investors say no, at least you faced your fear. And you understood that impact of making the right decision even if it means doing something you're afraid of. Because there is something greater than your fear. In this instance, it was a brighter financial future for you personally and for your business.

6. **Visualize the future with every decision:** We cannot stress visualization enough. It's important to imagine in your head the scene that can unfold with each decision you make. Try to tie in the emotion of it while you're at it. This will help you make a decision that may be a painful one. Also, if you feel that a certain decision doesn't feel so bad compared to the other, that's when you know that it could be the right one even if the outcome is rather sucky for you and the others.

7. **Get both sides of your brain involved:** Emotions and logic should come into account here. Engaging one side of your brain won't be enough. The goal here is to find a balance of emotion and reason with the decisions you make.

SECRETS USED BY NAVY SEALS & PROFESSIONAL ATHLETES TO DEVELOP UNBEATABLE SELF DISCIPLINE THAT MAKES DOING "HARD" TASKS INCREDIBLY EFFORTLESS

The US Navy SEALs are one of the most dangerous fighting forces in the known world. They have traveled the world over and taken part in missions where every decision they make was hard and complex.

Yet, they seem to make it look effortless by deciding the best course of action and acting on it. Professional athletes have a similar mindset that helps them make tough decisions look effortless. When the game is on the line and you're faced with a high-pressure situation, you need to be ready to make snap decisions that can result in winning the game or losing it.

You need to discipline yourself and resist the urge to crack under pressure or give up. You'll want to free yourself from the inability to press on. To quote what Jocko Wilinik said earlier, "discipline equals freedom". And Wilinik himself was a Navy SEAL, so he knows this very well.

We'll be taking a look at some of the secrets that both Navy SEALs and professional athletes know about making hard tasks as effortless as possible. Of course, it all boils down to self-discipline. They know things that we don't (until now). Here's what they are:

Start early

They say the early bird gets the worm. Those words can't be spoken with more truth. The task at hand must be done at some point during the day. You can't cut it too close before the deadline. The sooner you get it done, the better. Not to mention, you have more freedom to do what you want for the rest of the day. Starting early will give you more freedom so long as you don't procrastinate and waste time.

Stay in the moment

This is a big one. When you stay in the moment, you'll never lose sight of the prize. Don't look back and never look sideways. You'll get distracted and thrown off course. When you focus and keep it that way, you'll inch closer towards the goal without even caring how much time has elapsed and the like.

Take good care of yourself

Seems simple enough. You need to take care of yourself both mentally and physically. When you do, the two will work together in perfect harmony. When you do something that is physically challenging, your mind may play tricks on you if it's not completely aligned. You won't be able to manage the pain or endure the challenges that take a long time to complete. The key here is to keep pushing without killing yourself or going crazy.

Take care of your body, don't give into the bad habits and vices, and you will certainly give yourself peace of mind in knowing that you can accomplish whatever tasks you set forth. Also, keeping yourself in good shape physically can keep the mind sharp. Don't forget that.

Understand the importance of detail

Navy SEALs are known for their razor-sharp attention to detail. Everything needs to look perfect in its own way. Make your bed with no wrinkles. Anything that's the least bit crooked and you have to do it over again until you get it right. It's important that you focus on the details. Even the tiny ones. This doesn't mean you have to be a perfectionist. But you have to cover as many bases as possible. Nothing needs to be half-done. And subpar quality does not equal good enough.

Focus on one thing at a time

When you are putting in the practice, focus on one thing at a time. For example, if you are practicing for a presentation you can, do one slide at a time. Say what you need to say. Do it repeatedly before moving on. Do the same thing repeatedly over and over again and fine tune it if needed. Don't overload yourself. Focus on one thing and move onto the next. Rinse and repeat.

If you're surrounded by undisciplined people, do the opposite

Look around you. If you see a lot of people around you that are undisciplined, then do the exact opposite. Stand out above the rest of the "Herd". But when you are surrounded by people who are disciplined, that's when you work together. A lot of people decide to be undisciplined. But you don't have to be. Either you swim with the current or against it.

RECAP

Motivation is something that will come to you rather than something you have to find. Even if you have the motivation, it still won't be enough. You'll want to be able to have aspirations and dedication to compliment motivation. These are the building blocks that will create a potent mixture of discipline.

When it comes to your creativity, discipline should not even be part of the equation. Be creative and enjoy a different kind of freedom without submitting to the rules. Being creative is the only time where discipline is not needed.

If you are dealing with urges, it's important to ride the wave of urges instead of getting swallowed whole by it. Use the mindful technique we've outlined in the chapter. While you're at it, consider doing other things that will mentally reroute your thoughts rather than keep it stuck on the urge that you're trying to avoid. Don't fight it, but ride it instead of giving in.

Making decisions that are tough will need to be effortless. Only you can decide whether or not the decision is easy to swallow or harder than it needs to be. Use your instincts, consider the potential ramifications of each decision, and choose one that may have negative effects, but doesn't deliver a devastating blow to one's morale.

The secrets that Navy SEALs and pro athletes use that we've unveiled can be adapted into your life when disciplining yourself. Start early and ahead of the pack. Stay in the moment and keep at it no matter how tough it gets. Take the best care of yourself. Pay close attention to detail and make sure things look good. And always focus on one thing at a time when practicing. Take it slow and don't overload yourself with many things.

Developing discipline takes time. And it takes a good amount of strength and willpower to get through the obstacles that stand in the way. If you learn how to embrace the suck, you will make every "hard thing" a lot easier, even if it's painful to do.

8

STRENGTHENING MENTAL
TOUGHNESS

Now that you have a game plan to build discipline, we'll now focus on how you can strengthen your mental toughness. In this chapter, we will give you the ultimate guide on how you can build it up from start to finish. When it comes to discipline, mental toughness must exist to complement it.

Mental toughness is the same as physical toughness. In this context, it will take time and consistency to build up the strength. The more time you put into the gym, the stronger you become. With mental toughness, you can train yourself to handle the tough, high-pressure situations when others choose not to.

We'll give you some not so secret recipes on how to build mental toughness from the ground up. You'll learn what to include for the key ingredients that will cultivate into developing the strongest most fortified mentality you can put together. You can develop mental toughness, but not without a proven roadmap to get you from point A to point B. This chapter is exactly that.

Let's continue on with your journey:

THE NOT-SO-SECRET RECIPE FOR MENTAL TOUGHNESS

What we'll be taking a look at next is the not so secret recipe for mental toughness. These are the ingredients to living a mentally tough life. So long as you practice some of the following traits listed below, you will be able to maintain mental toughness for the rest of your days. Whether you are 30 or 60 years old, mental toughness lives on forever. Here are some of the ingredients that make up mental toughness:

- 1 complaint-free attitude
- 1-part mindfulness
- 1 full amount of control
- Dozens of self-respect and mindfulness
- 1-part talent
- 1-part ability
- Substitute bad habits with good strong habits
- Replace "yes" with "no"
- Substitute toxic people with your support network.

For best results, mix these ingredients and "slow cook" them for an unspecified amount of time. Don't worry about how long this will take you. The more you "cook" these ingredients together, the better your mental toughness will turn out and will last a long time.

Let's take a look in-depth as to why these ingredients should be included.

DON'T COMPLAIN

Complaining is a reflection of a poor attitude. There's no other way to say it. Especially when you complain about the trivial things. Someone who is mentally weak will often complain about the slightest changes. They will always look for things to complain about instead of finding the positive.

Not to mention, it's usually the things they can't control that they complain most about. The reality is that there is nothing you can do about it since it's way out of your hands.

KNOW THAT YOU HAVE CONTROL

We've said it before, and we'll say it again. The key to living with mental toughness is having control. You have control over your attitude, your fear, what you let in and what you let out. You can be able to control the things that will define you personally. Even if you feel like you're not in control, it's better to act as if you are than never at all.

MINDFULNESS IS KEY

Being mindful is one of the key components of mental toughness. You can take five minutes out of your day to meditate and remind yourself that you are in control of your thoughts. You can silence the noise in your mind when you take control of it. The more mindful you are, the better.

RESPECT YOURSELF

Those who respect themselves are often mentally tougher than those who don't. When you have respect for yourself, your self-talk will reflect that. No living person in the world can talk to themselves negatively and respect themselves at the same time. When it comes to self-talk, they are positive and use the right words subconsciously. Sometimes, they say it repeatedly in the form of affirmations, so it's embedded in their minds.

SELF-CONFIDENCE

Confidence is something that you must have in order to be mentally tough. You cannot seek it from outside sources (i.e. -- someone's opinion of you). To build self-confidence, you expose yourself to situations where you can be able to rise to the challenge, perform the necessary tasks, and complete them. The more "can do" that you have, the more confident you will become. It will put you on the path going from saying "I can't" to "I can".

HARNESSING YOUR EXISTING TALENT

Maybe you have an existing talent that you want to put to good use. And eventually, you want to improve it to keep yourself sharp. When you are mentally tough, you know that you have enough of the talent to perform the appropriate task. But no matter how good you are, usually there's always improvement to do better. Think of it like Windows. It's updated on a regular basis, even if it's something minor like ironing out a few bugs.

KNOW THAT YOU HAVE THE ABILITY

We've already covered about having the "can do" to perform a task. If you know that you have the ability, that gives you a boost in confidence. Even if you don't know how, give yourself the opportunity to learn. When you learn, you develop a skill that you can do on your own time. The more abilities you have, the more you can say "I can do that".

EMBRACING "NO"

Most people tend to view "no" as the devil. When in reality, it can be the most powerful word to say when you want to discipline yourself. Sure, there may be a negative emotion when you say no to the things you enjoy in favor of something that will benefit you in the long run. But in the end, you'll feel like you've made the right decision by saying no. It will become a lot easier to say "no" to things that are not important to you.

BE WILLING TO LEARN FROM YOUR MISTAKES

Everyone makes mistakes. No one is perfect. There is no other way to say it. And anyone who says otherwise is lying to you. But the real question is: how will you handle your mistakes? Those who are mentally tough acknowledge their mistakes, learn from them, and move on. The exact opposite of this is dwelling on them, complaining about them, and developing a fear to take action because they are afraid of making mistakes over and over again. Mistakes happen. Just be prepared to make them, embrace them, and dissect them for the purpose of learning from them.

TAKE RESPONSIBILITY FOR YOUR ACTIONS, WORDS, ETC.

It's mind-boggling to see that a lot of people don't take responsibility for their actions or what they say. They find the easy way out by blaming other people or things that are way beyond their control. These are the signs of mentally weak individuals. But you can be the exact opposite of this. When you screw up, it's important to approach it with the following attitude: "how can I make it better and what can be done so the same mistake isn't made again?"

ELIMINATE THE TOXIC PEOPLE FROM YOUR LIFE

If there is something that will throw you off your game, it's toxic people. They will spew negativity towards you. They could be bad mouthing or mocking someone else (or even you). You don't have time for that. Nor will you allow anyone to bring you down to their level. Cut them out of your life without shame. If it's so-called "friends", they'd be easy to dump. But if it's members of your family that are toxic, distance yourself from them as far as possible.

DESTROY YOUR BAD HABITS

Bad habits control our mentality for the worse. And it's easy for those to allow them to take control of us. You can't destroy your bad habits if you can't take control. Use the WOOP technique that you've learned early on in the book to break the bad habits and replace them with new ones. Develop good strong habits in their place. So long as you stay motivated and maintain consistency with these good habits, you'll do just fine.

FACT: IT IS EASY TO TELL SOMEONE TO BE POSITIVE, BUT DIFFICULT TO APPLY IT ON YOURSELF

For whatever reason, you can tell someone to be positive. However, you can't bring it to yourself to live by your own advice. That's kind of like telling someone to save their money so they can become a millionaire (but in reality, your money situation isn't the best). They tell you to be positive, but they never show you how to do it. This is where a lot of people end up failing. They don't have the road map to acquire that positive mindset.

Of course, you'll find exactly that in this book (and in this exact section as well). What you'll also get out of thinking positive are a lot of benefits both in the mental and physical sense. Those who live a positive life are less likely to develop certain health issues later on in their lifetime.

BE WISE IN DISTRIBUTING ENERGY

Distributing energy on tasks that are important will be essential. Especially when you need to get the tasks you need done. So, you do not want to focus on wasting energy on the activities that don't matter. This is why procrastination is such a momentum killer (not to mention an energy drainer). Sure, it's tempting to play video games or binge watch your favorite shows on Netflix. However, when you've finished the season finale, it would be hard for you to get started on the tasks that you were supposed to finish the day before.

When the day begins, focus on the critical tasks. When they are done, check your to do list to see what else can be done before the due date. Another thing, be sure to delegate any tasks that may not require your energy since you have other things to focus on.

THE TRUTH ABOUT WILLPOWER, AND HOW TO APPLY THIS KNOWLEDGE TO YOUR ADVANTAGE

What you need to know about willpower is that it is something that you will be exercising for much of your journey. Discipline and mental toughness will rely on willpower more often than not. If you can resist the urge to not get distracted, only then will you be able to harness the true willpower that is inside you. Remember, a lot of us have willpower inside of ourselves. But the only difference is that there are two kinds of people: those who are willing to tap into that supply of willpower and those who are not able to do so (because they don't know it yet).

In a later chapter, we will show you a prime example of willpower in what is known as delayed gratification. We'll explain exactly what that is and how it ties into willpower.

HONING YOUR TALENTS AND ABILITIES TO ITS BEST FORM

Your talents and abilities can be upgraded to its best form. The more you practice them to make them even better, the more you will be able to put them to good use when it comes to achieving the tasks you are good at. This will not only reinforce your confidence in doing things flawlessly, but it will ensure that you have the mental toughness to perform your abilities and talents at the highest level. You know that even if there is little room for error, you'll be able to get the job done without fail.

You can improve your skills at the current level you're at right now and be better. You may be happy with your current skill level, but there may always be room for improvement no matter what.

YOUR CONFIDENCE STARTS WITHIN, NOT ON WHAT SOMEBODY ELSE SAYS

When it comes to confidence, no one can produce it better than you. It is unnecessary to rely on external sources. What we mean by this is this: it's a complete waste of time to try and seek approval from other people. Others' opinions of you should not define your level of confidence. Your abilities and talents do. If you can get the job done, you know you can do it again. You have the confidence to perform the same task over and over again and produce great results in the process.

People will speak highly of you and have your opinion of you in a positive light. You can graciously accept that. But if someone criticizes you negatively, you can choose to ignore it or let it dampen your spirits and confidence. It would be smart of you to ignore the naysayers and keep pressing on as if you never heard it.

USE MENTAL TOUGHNESS TO DEVELOP LASTING HEALTHY AND POSITIVE HABITS IN ALL AREAS OF LIFE

Mental toughness is needed when you want to focus on all aspects in your life. Whether it's with physical fitness, your abilities and talents, or being a better friend or family member using mental toughness to better yourself and building good habits will be effective. You can build habits that will not only focus on one area, but it can also be connected to other areas of your life as well. With a healthy lifestyle thanks to positive habits, it can also allow you to live longer and therefore give you more time to spend with your family. That alone will also help you strengthen your bond with those who are important people in your life.

EMBRACING YOUR IMPERFECTIONS

Whether we're born with them or not, imperfections are a blessing in disguise. Some of these imperfections are things that we cannot control. And that's OK. The best that you can do is see the positive in the potential negative. Rather than let imperfections get the best of you, you keep doing your best. Now, people may talk negatively about your imperfections and say that you can't do such things because of them. But it's all talk. And only the mentally tough with imperfections do not allow that negativity to get the best of them.

MORE SECRETS FROM NAVY SEALS & PROFESSIONAL ATHLETES THAT YOU SHOULD PUT INTO USE

As promised, we'll be taking a look at more secrets from Navy SEALs and professional athletes that will help you become more mentally tough. Earlier, we've discussed that discipline equals freedom. The Navy SEALs have a motto that they live by on a daily basis. The motto is "The Easy Day Was Yesterday". Sure enough, each day can be more challenging than the last. For this reason, you can expect the next day to present you with even tougher challenges. Because the next day will be a lot harder compared to the last.

One other secret that we want to share is something that Navy SEALs still use to this day. This is known as the "40 percent rule". The rule states that when you feel tapped out after getting 40 percent of the work done, know that you have 60 percent left in the tank. Even if you are tapped out, you have it within you to finish what you started. There is no quit in you. If you ever think about quitting, don't.

THERE'S A GOOD KIND OF STRESS THAT YOU SHOULD USE

Did you know that there are two kinds of stress out there? There is good stress (eustress) and bad stress (distress). Of course, you need to use the good stress to your advantage. The reason why is that it will give you an energy boost to keep going, even when the pressure is on. Though it is short-term, it will be exactly what you need to speed on through the home stretch. How long does it last? It's anyone's guess. But as long as you use it to get the tasks done, nothing can stop you.

Distress on the other hand will derail you and cause you to crack under pressure. This kind of stress can be short-term, but it can be long-term if you keep on dragging it out.

9

KEEP CALM AND ...

The best way to boost your discipline and mental toughness is the ability to remain calm. This chapter will be dedicated to helping you keep a calm mind so you can achieve a new level of mindfulness that is essential. The calmer you are, the more disciplined you will be. Your levels of calm will also be a barometer for your mental toughness overall.

We'll show you ways to relax, how you can incorporate meditation, and how to become more mindfully aware of yourself at all times. This is a chapter you really should not skip (and for good reason). Without a calm mind, you'll be stressed all the time. And you'll allow yourself to apply more pressure than you already need to. Those who are undisciplined and not mentally tough will crack at a moment's notice.

By the end of this chapter, you'll have a few tricks up your sleeve on how to keep calm and carry on as they say. Doing so will help you achieve as many personal victories as you can. Let's dive right in and begin this chapter talking about relaxation.

RELAX

It's important to know how to relax. When you relax, your body won't feel as tense. Internal organs like your heart and lungs won't work too hard because you are not under amounts of stress. People tell us to relax like they know a thing or two. Maybe they do. But the reality is telling ourselves and others to relax is easy enough. It's the actual doing that can be difficult for many.

Relaxation techniques are much needed for a lot of us who face stressful situations on a regular basis. You'll learn a few of these in this section and find out why they are important. Some of these techniques will be your "go-to" options. If you keep doing them consistently, you'll be able to perform them like it's second nature. Here are some of our favorite relaxation techniques that we recommend:

Write it down: Keeping a journal is highly suggested. Especially when you want to develop discipline and mental toughness. In this instance, you want to write down what's bothering you. Take your thoughts and issues and put them to the paper (or in a Word doc if that's your thing). Take a few minutes out of the day to write out what comes to mind. What's bothering you? What can you do to solve the problem? Just you and your thoughts. No one but yourself will see it.

Just breathe: Later on in the chapter, we're going to go over a few breathing exercises. Having these on hand will really separate you from the pack. You can take a moment to find a quiet space so you can perform these breathing techniques. They can be in your workspace, in the bathroom, or someplace quiet where no one can bother you.

Make a gratitude list: Write down as many as five things that you are thankful for. This can be done in a daily journal entry or in a separate notebook. When writing down the things that you are grateful for, your mind is drawn back down to Earth. You'll come to the realization that you're thankful for what you got. Plus, it allows you to mentally focus on the positive as opposed to the negative.

Stretch it out: Stretches are one of the best ways to keep the muscles free of any tension. This can be basic stretches. Or you can take it a step further and do some yoga (which we will talk about later on in the chapter). Relaxation is mostly mental, but there are some physical aspects to it as well. Remember, stress can not only take a toll on you mentally but also physically.

Take it outside: It can be a nice sunny day outside and a bit warm as well. Sounds like the perfect day to go for a walk and get some fresh air. It's one of the perfect environments where you can relax and enjoy yourself. If you live in an area that is cold during the wintertime, you can take walks if you bundle up and can handle the chilly temperatures (but keep it short).

Relaxation gives you plenty of benefits. One major benefit that we're aiming for is the ability to think clearly and make better decisions without involving a high level of emotion. You can be able to solve problems with ease when you can think clear thoughts. You'll be able to get a 10,000-foot view of what decision will be the better of the two. If they are tough with some negative results at either end, you'll take the time to assess which option will yield the lesser amount of "pain".

As mentioned before, your physical health will benefit. When you're relaxed, you'll be able to enjoy health benefits such as keeping your blood pressure at lower levels. You'll also reduce your risk of heart attacks and autoimmune illnesses. Relaxation is good for the body and mind. There's no better way to say it.

CONCENTRATION

Knowing how to concentrate (even when it's "on demand") can be tricky. When you need to perform tasks that warrant your full undivided attention, concentration will be hard to come by. Lucky for you, we have some tricks up our sleeve that will help you acquire a new level of concentration that your friends and colleagues will envy you for.

When you have an improved level of concentration, you'll easily find yourself "in the zone" and get the tasks done. Wasting time will be the last thing you'll ever think of doing. In this section, we'll show you tips on how you can improve your concentration and focus. Along with that, we'll show you some of our favorite exercises that are guaranteed to help you concentrate even on the days when things can get very hectic.

Once you are able to concentrate and focus with the help of these exercises, you'll seem unstoppable. And you'll be able to keep the momentum going even on days when the daily task list is building up.

9 TIPS ON IMPROVING CONCENTRATION AND FOCUS

Without wasting any more time, let's take a look at the nine tips that you should take to heart when it comes to improving concentration and focus:

1. Get rid of distractions

As if this wasn't said enough times. Distractions kill concentration and focus in an instant. At this point, you should have a good idea on how to get rid of them. If you seem to experience a "slip of the mind" (don't worry, it happens), then go back to Chapter 3 where it talks about distractions and how to minimize them.

2. Focus on one thing at a time

Sure, people will brag about how they are the best multi-taskers in the world. We probably envy them. However, it's not smart to try to keep up with them. Sometimes, those who brag about being great multi-taskers can get into even bigger messes. But not you, though. You can focus on one thing at a time. When you focus on a single task, the quality and performance will be much better.

3. Take stock of your mental focus

Assessing your mental focus doesn't take a lot of time and effort. But you'll be able to know the difference between having it and lacking it. If you lose track of what you're doing or get easily distracted, it's clear that you'll need to work on it. If you manage to stay alert and take short breaks without dragging it out for too long, your mental focus should be right where it's at.

4. Be in the moment

When you're in the moment, you'll focus better. You don't focus on the past or the future. You are focusing on right now. In fact, consider the "past" and "future" things as glorified distractions. Don't worry about the "what ifs". Don't focus on past failures that will throw you off your game. When you tune your mind out of those things, you have no choice but to focus on what's right in front of you.

5. Take a short break

Sometimes, you deserve a break from what you're working on. You don't want to overwork yourself to the point where your focus and concentration evaporates. If you use a timer or use the Pomodoro technique, set a timer for how long you want to perform your task. After time runs out, take a short break ranging from 10 to 15 minutes. Once you allow yourself to re-group mentally, pick up where you left off. Also, resist the urge of getting too distracted on your breaks. A 15-minute break could stretch out to 30 minutes (which could get stretched to an hour).

6. Do light, physical activities

Tying into number five, you should use your break time as the perfect opportunity to do some light physical exercises. This can be a brisk walk around the block or finding a place to pound out some sit-ups and pushups. Or maybe there's a flight of stairs you can climb up and down to keep yourself in shape. You can keep your body and mind in good shape all at the same time. All it takes is 5 to 15 minutes.

7. Exercise your mind

Think that physical exercise is enough? Well, it wouldn't be fair to leave your brain out of the mix now, would it? Exercising your mind and keeping it strong will definitely help with concentration and focus. You can consider doing tried and true methods like crossword puzzles or similar games that you'll find in newspapers or booklets. Before you say anything, those brain games that you see online and on mobile apps may be fun to play. However, the jury is still out on whether or not they are beneficial to improving your focus. So, err on the side of brain exercises that don't require a lot of technology.

8. Don't TL; DR

You see that TL; DR all the time online. "Too long, didn't read" has become the norm for most people these days. So, most people would rather go for the executive summary of things rather than read it as a whole. But those who decide to read, and study lengthy pieces of writing will have more of an edge in terms of focus. Not to mention, it will help train your mind to absorb more information like a sponge.

9. Always keep practicing

Improving your focus and concentration is not some one-off thing. You do it over and over again. That's why it's always important to have a plan. Take regular breaks, reduce distractions, focus on one thing at a time no matter how long it takes. Practice does make perfect. And it will also help you become more in tune and focused compared to most people.

These nine tips will be helpful in making sure that your brain is on the right track when it comes to concentration and focus. Being able to deal with less distractions while focusing on just one single task are just two of the things you have to incorporate in your life if you want to make improvements. But that doesn't mean you have to ignore the other tips listed.

BE MINDFUL AND DEVELOP AWARENESS

Mindfulness is talked about a lot lately. However, a lot of people don't seem to get the message. Mindfulness is helpful whenever you want to develop a new level of self-awareness. Self-awareness is the ability where you know what you're doing. And it can be helpful in catching yourself when you're doing things that may be considered distractions.

We'll be taking a look at ways where you can develop mindfulness every single day. Not only will you be able to stop for a moment and gather your thoughts before continuing forward, you'll be able do this "on demand" whenever it seems hard to come by. Here are some things you'll want to do:

Practice mindfulness the moment you wake up: Being able to practice mindfulness the second you wake up is a must. It can be a quick five-minute meditation before you move on with the rest of the day. If for some reason you find yourself falling back asleep, you may want to consider drinking a cup of coffee or caffeinated tea before you do your mindfulness exercise.

Pay attention while doing routine things: As ridiculous as it sounds, paying attention to how you do routine things will help open up a part of your brain that is not often accessed because of our brain's "autopilot" feature. Focus on the sight, sound, taste, and feel of the activities that you normally do. Your autopilot feature will blunt these senses. But if you really focus on them, you'll probably uncover some interesting things about them.

Keep your mindfulness sessions short: Short mindfulness sessions will help keep your mind sharp and flexible. You can start out by doing a five-minute interval. Work your way up to 15 minutes max. Don't go any longer than it has to be. When you have short mindfulness sessions, it's a lot better than taking a week off just to relax.

Practice mindfulness in some stressful situations: When things get stressful, our brains get cranked into overdrive. While most will focus on taking out their frustrations on something or someone, you'll be a step above them. If you're waiting on the phone for a lengthy period (that on-hold music can be annoying), you can practice mindfulness exercises while you're waiting. The same if you are stuck in a traffic jam. Keep it short and sweet (as suggested in the previous tip) and stay in the moment. These stressful moments will pass whether you know it or not.

Meditation is your friend: Meditation is by far one of the best ways to achieve total mindfulness. Thankfully, we'll be talking more about it in the next section. Doing this on a daily basis will help you set the tone throughout the day. It can kill off any self-doubt and negative talk. Once you are present and able to keep a calm mind, you'll be saying things a lot differently. So instead of saying "this day is going to suck", you can say "this day will be stressful, but I have what it takes to handle it".

MEDITATE

Now, we get to the fun part. You cannot necessarily achieve complete and total mindfulness if you don't meditate. Before we go any further, meditation is not going to cause any kind of "depersonalization" or the like. But you'll feel like an entirely different person once you get the hang of it and experience some awesome short-term and long-term benefits.

We'll show you how to meditate the right way so you can do it for five minutes or even a half hour. Also, since meditation does require concentration, you'll want to pay close attention to these instructions. This way, you'll know exactly what to do without having to rely on written instructions. Alternatively, you can record the following steps below and put together a guided meditation.

Let's take a deep breath...and dive right in:

1. Get comfortable

First things first, you want to make sure that you are able to get comfortable. You'll also want to get it to a point where you can be able to sit still for a few minutes straight. At this point, the only thing you'll need to focus on is your breathing. In...and out.

2. Focus on the breath

At this point, you'll want to focus even more on your breathing. Where do you feel it the most? As you are breathing in and out (and continue to do so), see if you feel it most in your belly or through your nose.

3. Follow the breath

To do this, breathe in through the nose for as long as possible. As you do this, expand your belly. You can hold for a couple of seconds before exhaling slowly. Make sure the out breath is long and slow. Be sure to contract your belly while doing this. Start by doing this for at least two minutes and work your way up to longer periods whenever you feel comfortable.

And there you have it. You now know how to meditate in three easy steps. Pretty cool, huh? When you try this out, it will feel like an experience unlike any other. You might not get enough of it. However, you should consider doing this for a shorter period of time (even when done multiple times throughout the day).

BREATHE

Believe it or not, there is more than one way to breathe. In this section, you'll learn about some of the best tips about different breathing techniques and how you can do certain exercises whether you are sitting or laying down. Either way, this will help you get more in tune with your body so you can pay even closer attention to how you breathe.

Now, let's get you into becoming an "expert" on breathing. While most people will breathe on autopilot (because you have to), let's take a look at ways to control it so you are more in tune with your mind. Here we go:

The Navy SEAL breathing technique for maximum focus: If there is one more thing we can learn from the Navy SEALs, it's a breathing technique that will help them focus while they are on death defying missions. The first thing you do is breathe in slowly while expanding your belly. At the top of the breath, hold for four seconds. Exhale and contract your belly for four seconds. Then hold on the down breath for another four seconds and repeat the process.

Use your diaphragm to breathe: Remember when we said that you should breathe in and expand your belly? Well, keep doing that. Because you've just learned how to breathe from your diaphragm. Not only does this make breathing easier, but it also makes it less of a chore for your lungs to help you breathe. It will also strengthen your diaphragm in the process. Also, you may notice that your voice may become deeper or more powerful. That alone can make you more of someone who is viewed as authority. Just make sure you have the discipline and mental toughness to compliment it.

Do breathing exercises regularly: We'll be taking a look at two breathing exercises shortly. What you'll need to do is perform one of these for five to ten minutes per day. It's important to focus on your breathing and learn how to breathe from your diaphragm instead of breathing from your chest.

BREATHING EXERCISES TO TRY

We will be trying two different breathing exercises: one while you're sitting and the other while you're laying down. You can start out with either one of these. If you are a total beginner, try doing it for at least five minutes. You can work your way up to ten minutes if you feel more comfortable to make adjustments.

Let's start with the sitting down breathing exercise:

Breathing Exercise While Sitting

- Sit in a comfortable position. Make sure your knees are bent.
- Make sure you are completely relaxed. This includes your head, neck, and shoulders.
- Next, place one of your hands on top of your chest. The other hand will need to be placed below your rib cage. This will allow you to feel the movement of your diaphragm while you breathe.
- As you slowly inhale through the nose, make sure that your

stomach is pressed up against your hand. While doing this, make sure that your hand on your chest remains still.

- Exhale through your lips (while pursed). Make sure your hand on your chest remains still.
- Repeat the process for five to ten minutes.

Breathing Exercise While Laying Down

- Lie on your back with your knees bent. To ensure better support for your legs, place a pillow or two underneath your knees.
- Hand placement is the same. One on your chest and the other on you beneath your rib cage.
- Breathe in through the nose while your stomach presses against your hand. The hand on your chest must remain still.
- Breathe out the mouth (pursed) lips. Keep your hand on your chest still.
- Repeat the process for five to ten minutes.

When starting out, you'll try out both exercises to determine which of the two are the most comfortable. The laying down technique is slightly more difficult since you'll be on your back. Try each version once and decide which one will work best for you. As you probably notice, the technique is basically the same.

The main goal of these breathing exercises is to make sure you are breathing with your diaphragm as opposed to your chest. If the hand on your chest moves while you are breathing, you are not breathing through your diaphragm. It does take a bit of focus and practice to pull this off. And that's why we require you to practice this a few times a week.

Even after you are able to do this with little to no effort, it never hurts to keep doing it just to keep your breathing in check. Especially when you are meditating and keeping your mindfulness sharp.

THINK & DO ZEN

The focus of doing Zen is defined as centering your attention to the task at hand (which is basically what we're aiming to do). Believe it or not, Zen is a discipline. You don't have to be religious or commit yourself to Buddhism to know and use Zen to your advantage. Zen meditation is another opportunity to tune your mindfulness for the better.

But you can learn from the Zen discipline in order to achieve total mindfulness. You can meditate regularly. Focus on your breathing while clearing your mind. As mentioned before, Zen is all about discipline. It's about restraining yourself from what would possibly throw you off mentally and physically.

The Zen philosophy teaches you to be aware and in the moment. And when you are able to know that you're in the moment, the past and the future don't seem to matter. You'll be able to focus on the task at hand without caring about your past failures or worrying about future ones.

LEARN YOGA

Yoga is one of the best stress busters out there. Not only will it help improve your body physically, but it's also one of the best ways to keep your mind sharp so you are disciplined and mentally tough. While several schools of yoga exist, the concept is pretty much the same.

You can learn yoga by simply searching online for guides and videos on how to perform basic yoga poses. Also, if there's a yoga studio in your local area, be sure to see if there are some regular classes that are coming up. A basic yoga class might help in terms of helping you improve yourself in both body and mind.

BEGINNERS POSES YOU CAN TRY OUT

If you are a complete beginner at yoga, we'll show you a few poses that you can try at home. These are easy to do, and they won't cause you to twist and tie yourself up like a pretzel. You can do these anywhere as long as you have enough space and have a place where no one can bother you. Alternatively, you can get a few people to do some quick yoga with you so they too can beat the stress that gets thrown at them during the day.

Let's get right to the list:

1. Mountain pose

The mountain pose is the basic yoga pose. It's so simple that anyone can do it. What you need to do is stand up straight with your feet together. Your arms should be to your side. So, in other words, you're basically standing.

However, we're not done yet. Next, you want to squeeze your quads, so your kneecaps are lifted. You'll also want to draw in your abdominal muscles while lifting your chest and pressing down your shoulders. Also, try to put your shoulder blades as close together as possible. Make sure your palms are facing inward and lift your head up as if it's being pulled by a string. Hold this pose for five breaths (work your way up to eight breaths when you become more comfortable).

2. Plank

The plank is the perfect yoga pose whenever you want to work on your balance. While it's a simple pose, it's a bit physically challenging. In order to do this, get on all fours. Assume the "up" position as if you're about ready to do a push-up. Pull in the lower abdominals and pull the shoulders as far from your ears as possible. Pull in your ribs and hold the pose for five breaths.

3. Tree

This one requires a bit more balance. But unlike the Plank, you'll be in a standing position. However, here's the challenge: you'll need to stand on one foot. It doesn't matter which one. Lift one foot and cross it over the leg like you are making a "4". Stay standing in that position and hold for five breaths.

4. Child's Pose

For this last pose, this one will work to perfection whenever you need to get rid of tension and stress. What you'll need to do is get on your knees and lean forward so you are in a prone position. Tuck your knees into your chest and stomach. Then stretch your arms forward. You can allow your head to touch the floor or elevate it with a pillow. Hold the pose for as long as you like.

These are just a sample of the many poses that exist in yoga. But these four are the basic ones you can try right now if you like. Also, you should use a yoga mat whenever you want to try out these poses. That way, you won't have to rely on a floor that may be dirty or disgusting.

RECAP

Being able to keep calm and relaxed is all part of being disciplined and mentally tough. Especially when you want to achieve a high level of mindfulness. Mindfulness isn't just meditation alone. It can be focusing on routine things and going past your autopilot to really get a feel of the senses that go into things like brushing your teeth.

Meditation is important and you should do it for at least a few minutes a day. Not only will it allow you to clear out any stress and tension you may have, it will help you get through the day even when the going gets tough. Also, it wouldn't hurt to do some breathing exercises so you can be able to breathe through your diaphragm more and less with your chest.

It's important to instill some kind of discipline the same way those who practice Zen do. You can do this without being spiritual or converting to the Buddhist religion. The Zen philosophy has a ton of examples that will help you on the journey towards complete mindfulness.

Finally, take some time out of your day to do some regular yoga poses. They don't have to be complicated. The basics will do just fine even when you're starting out. It's possible to become more mindful than you are now. Having this power will separate you over many others around you. Mindfulness leads to a clear mind, better decision making, and handling almost any stressful situation.

BREAKING OLD ROUTINES AND CREATING EFFECTIVE HABITS

I f there is one tenant that is key to living a more disciplined life, it's all about adopting good effective habits. This chapter will be the ultimate roadmap towards breaking bad habits while instilling good ones in the process. It's true what they say: a bad habit is easy to form but very hard to break. With good habits, it's the other way around for most.

When the going gets tough and things get stressful, what bad habits are your go-to "comforts"? Do you smoke? Do you eat? What is your automatic response that stress can trigger? Or better yet, what is that trigger that will lead you to respond automatically to performing a bad routine you want to break.

You will learn how to form these good habits as if it were easy to do. Those who adopt good habits are usually more disciplined and mentally tough. Because their "can do" attitude will help them go from point A to point B no matter how long it takes. The debate about how long a habit can take to form is still debatable. But as long as you stay the course and form good habits (while watching your old routines disappear in the rear-view mirror, you'll be golden).

Now, let's finally say goodbye to those old habits that represent a lack of discipline and mental toughness:

THE STRUGGLE OF STICKING TO VALUABLE HABITS

Why is a good habit so hard to form? That's the million-dollar question. We may or may not finally have the answer to this question that has stumped many over the years. One of the main reasons why a good habit is so hard to form is because it's not as "attractive" as a bad habit. Attraction is not a word that ties into finding that significant other. Any habit that is considered "attractive" is something that will likely stick to a person for a longer period of time. Not to mention, the "reward" of exercising that habit will also further justify the decision to do it once (and then do it repeatedly when the need arises).

When there's a small region of attraction for a habit (like some good habits), then odds are the likelihood of that forming into something long-lived won't be good. In fact, it could have a 1 percent chance of surviving. However, there are ways to expand that region of attraction for good habits. That's performing the habit over and over again until it becomes a routine thing.

However, there's one thing to point out: someone who adopts a good habit expects to get it right on the first try. If they screw up, they throw their hands up and say "whatever, it was worth a shot". However, being consistent with a habit to a point where it becomes more attractive to do it because of the short-term and long-term rewards are what we're gunning for here.

For example, let's take a look at working out here. You know that the goal is losing weight. But you want to keep it as simple as possible. So, you purchase a kettlebell, learn a few workouts, and crank them out for about 20 minutes a day. You'll feel great, have more energy, and want to get it done the next time. No need to worry about "moving" parts or waiting for someone to leave the lifting station at the gym. If the conditions are right, you can form a good habit with little to no effort.

Why do you suppose we chose a kettlebell in this example instead of say regular weights? With a kettlebell, you just pick it up and start lifting. With regular weights, you have to walk to the plate rack, add the weights to the bar, lift, and so on. That may seem a bit complicated for someone, especially if they're actually crunched for time.

Also, one deviation from the initial conditions will also throw them off course. And that can throw a wrench into their plans of developing a good habit. When they see diminishing returns, they can either give up or level up. You can go from a 25-pound kettlebell to a 35-pound kettlebell or stop lifting altogether. What appears to be the best option for you in this situation?

Another key to forming a habit is repetition. You do the same thing over and over again. As tedious as it is, you keep doing it. The reward of being able to do the same thing without fail will help you form that good habit. Sure, there will be challenges and roadblocks. So, you must mentally expect them to happen. At the same time, it's important to stay focused and keep your eye on the prize.

DON'T RUSH! YOU CAN TAKE THE PATH OF SLOWLY BUT SURELY

Do you remember the legendary story of "The Tortoise and The Hare"? If you do, you know that "slow and steady" wins the race. Sure, the hare was fast and had an excellent speed advantage than the tortoise. However, the hare's complacency is one of the reasons why he lost. Meanwhile, the tortoise took his time and kept going.

The point is that when forming a new habit, it really doesn't matter how long it takes. But one thing is for sure, once you form a good habit you don't want to be complacent and forget about it. Also, you don't want to rush into forming a good habit either. Because the quality and longevity of the habit itself will be poor (and you'll fall back into old habits again).

Think about building a new habit like you're building a new skyscraper. It's a building that will change the city skyline for a long time. You are competing against a rival builder who wants to build a tower that is designed to be bigger and better. Your rival said that he can get it done faster than you (and you may not stand a chance to beat him). But you build yours anyways, brick by brick.

You are slowly but surely building the tower because the little things will add up over time. The building will get taller. And it will be more stable as it goes. You look over the little details and make some changes when necessary. When the building is finished, it stands strong and looks majestic. It may have taken a year to do it (which may not be the case for most habits), but the important thing was you took your time.

Meanwhile, your rival finished his tower in six months. He said he was going to get it done faster than you. Yes, it's bigger than yours. But it ain't better in terms of structural integrity. When a light wind began to blow, his tower began to crumble and collapse. Obviously, rushing into something will cause you to overlook some of the smallest possible details that are critical to forming a habit.

The moral of this story is that when performing the smaller tasks, it is less likely for you to resist the idea of doing it again and again. And that's the key to building a good habit. Where many fail to build a good habit simply boils down to getting the results fast and in a hurry. However, when they see that it's not like that, they call it pointless and give up. They need to accept the fact that it takes small steps or small blocks to build a good habit. And no matter how long it takes, they'll get there so long as they keep at it.

10 SIMPLE, YET INCREDIBLY EFFECTIVE, STRATEGIES FOR DEVELOPING POSITIVE HABITS IN ALL REALMS OF LIFE (IT'S MUCH EASIER THAN YOU THINK)

Below are ten of the simple and effective strategies to help you develop positive habits. These will be useful for all kinds of habits in every aspect of your life. Adopting these will make forming good habits a lot easier. People may envy you and some may even ask you "can you teach me how"? Either way, it's a good feeling knowing that you will be armed with a battle plan to form good habits.

Let's take a look at the first one:

1. Start out small

This can't be said better than this. Starting out small is a lot better than "going big or going home". It takes one small step to get started. It takes another small step to continue. Remember, small steps will likely get you to take another one. Don't feel like you have to make giant steps to go from one point to the next.

2. Set a small goal

Setting small goals will likely put you on the path towards forming a better habit. At the start, you should commit to 30 days to form a good habit. Some say it may be all you need to form a good habit to begin with. As we've mentioned before, the actual timing is a matter of dispute. A month may be easier to sustain for most. But if it's a bit of a challenge, you could get away with breaking it down to a smaller time frame like 7 to 14 days. After that time frame, reset the goal and do it again.

3. Remind yourself

Circling back to the last statement in number two, it's important to remind yourself to reset the timeframe that you set for forming a habit. So, if you commit to thirty days, set a reminder. When the reminder goes off, you'll know it's time to re-commit to another thirty and do it again. As tedious as it is, repetition is key in building a good habit.

4. Consistency is key

One of the true cornerstones of building a good habit is consistency. If you decide to work out for a span of 30 days, set an exact time on when to start doing it. 30 days of working out starting at 6AM will be the perfect recipe for building a habit. Because setting a specific time will be a "cue" to get you to act almost on autopilot. Speaking of which...let's talk more about "cues" or its original name in the next item on the list.

5. Form triggers

A trigger is defined as a ritual that you perform before you act on a certain habit. However, a trigger can be a set of conditions that will be perfect for a habit (good or bad). No matter how ridiculous it has to be (like snapping your fingers if you need a cigarette), a trigger will help you act on a good habit or break a bad one. As long as you follow through with it, you're golden.

6. Find a good replacement

If you are breaking a bad habit, then it's important to find something good to replace it. For example, if you are drinking soda but want to rely on caffeine to get you through the morning, consider replacing it with coffee instead. Remember to keep in mind the kind of values you want to retain (or risk losing) when breaking a bad habit and replacing it with a good one. If you place caffeine at a high value, don't deprive yourself of it when breaking that bad habit. There are more than enough ways to form a good habit while keeping your values intact.

7. Don't strive for perfection

As mentioned before, many people give up forming good habits because they expect to get it right and perfect the first time. Accept the fact that you will make mistakes and have a few stumbling blocks to cross over. What matters is that you keep going and correct any mistakes along the way.

8. Get an accountability buddy

Sometimes, relying on technology to remind you to keep going won't be enough. So, it's important to find someone you trust to help keep you accountable. It can be a parent, a sibling, or your best friend. Any one of these people who you highly value and trust are the people you want as an accountability buddy. It can be someone who wants to form the same good habits as you.

9. Eliminate the temptations

Are you losing weight but there is plenty of junk food in the cupboards? Throw them out. Are you spending money on something that isn't giving you a good return on investment? Cancel it. There are plenty of temptations that you can easily eliminate. Doing so will help you stay focused on that good habit without having to relapse bad into your old way.

10. Know the benefits

Knowing what the benefits are at all times will keep you going. It's also important to visualize what will happen if you stick with it (while doing the same in terms of what if you decide not to form a good habit). Where will you see yourself in six months to a year? Will you be feeling better knowing you have a few good habits? Or will it be the same old, same old?

FIND 'POSITIVE BEHAVIORS' AND HABITS THAT YOU CAN ACTUALLY ENJOY AND LOOK FORWARD TO

Looking for positive behaviors and habits that you are more than looking forward to are what disciplined, and mentally tough people always do. For them, it's as easy and effortless like ordering their favorite pizza. We'll be looking at some of the behaviors and habits that most people who are mentally tough and disciplined perform very well. You too when you decide to take them on yourself.

Here are just a few of those habits that you'll see from those types of people (and what you will likely do as well):

Know the distinction between letting go and giving up

Letting go is not the same as giving up. Here's an example of that. Let's say your ultimate goal is to have a prosperous and successful career. You decide that being a doctor is that best course of action. After you go through your undergraduate studies and apply to medical school, you figured that it may be time to go through the motions once more. Then one day, you decide that maybe being a doctor isn't what you really want to do.

However, you've had quite a deep interest in law for years. You love talking about it and you obsess over Supreme Court cases of historic proportions. So, you decide to drop out of med school in favor of law school. This is an example of letting go of something, not giving up. You've just created another way to get to your ultimate goal while letting go of the old way.

Giving up is basically just dropping the goal altogether. See the difference?

They are in total control

Simple enough, right? Those who are mentally tough are in control no matter how chaotic the situation is. They don't focus on the things that are beyond themselves. Focus on the things you can control and worry less about the things that you can't.

Eliminate the things that have no impact or value

Again, another simple thing to do. If it's a waste of time or it provides a negative return on value, get rid of it. This includes cutting out toxic people, canceling subscriptions that are a waste of money, and eliminating things you don't seem to have the time to focus on anymore.

Focus on impressing yourself

This may sound selfish or arrogant. But focusing on impressing yourself is a lot better than trying to impress others (and come off as some try hard). Besides, why should you vie for the approval of others when you can focus on something that you yourself will approve?

MORE AND MORE PEOPLE ARE USING THIS SELF-DISCIPLINE AND HABIT-FORMING SYSTEM

Lastly, we'll be taking a look at a simple to use habit forming system that will help you become more disciplined and be able to form a good habit no matter what it is. Without wasting time, let's get right to it:

Identify the routine

There are three things to a routine: the cue, the routine, and the reward. If it's a bad routine, you'll need to consider what's causing you to act on it. Also, you'll want to identify the reward when the routine itself is completed. Keep in mind that the long-term effects of the rewards may not be as good as you think.

Identify the cue

What is that cue or trigger that is getting you to perform that routine. If you have more than one cue, write them down on a piece of paper. Is it a certain mood that triggers it? Is it a specific environmental condition (i.e.-- you're home alone)? What time is it? What is your current mood? There are various conditions and the like that will make up the entire cue.

When it comes to good habits, create a cue that will help you execute on it. If it's a bad habit, know what the cue is and isolate it. You'll know exactly what the causes are for these bad habits by time, behavior, and the like.

Know the rewards

If you are trying to lose weight, then you know that the reward is living a healthy lifestyle. But it goes beyond that. People like to go a little deeper in their thought process. A healthier lifestyle means more time with their families, living a long healthy life, and a chance to do the things they want to do even in their golden years. The rewards go a lot deeper than you think.

RECAP

Breaking old habits and forming new ones can finally be a lot easier. There is no need for you to make giant leaps or expect the perfect results on the first try. The key here is to start small and start slow. Never mind about the timing. Never rush as it will increase the likelihood of giving up on a good habit too early.

It's important to follow the simple and effective strategies of building a habit. That way, when there's a good habit you want to adopt, you can be able to get it done with ease. Plus, you'll want to instill some habits that are used by mentally tough and disciplined individuals. Knowing that you're in control and being able to distinguish between letting go and giving up among other habits will put you well above the others around you.

Finally, you can put together a simple formula that will help you form a good habit (while eliminating a bad one) simply by identifying the routine and cues. Plus, knowing what the rewards are and looking deep beyond them will be a key factor in deciding whether the habit is good enough to form or bad enough to make changes.

11

OVERCOMING PROCRASTINATION AND MAKING FRIENDS WITH TIME

Procrastination is one of the worst habits that anyone can have. It's easy for us to put things off until later on in favor of things we actually enjoy. However, in reality procrastination will add more pressure on you when timing is certainly not a factor. The more you have to get done when it's so close to the deadline, the greater the pressure. And that could be enough to get you to crack under pressure mentally.

This chapter will show you how to overcome procrastination and be able to enlist time as your greatest ally rather than your worst enemy. The truth is, time can really do you a favor if you manage it just right. You'll learn time management skills that you can adopt as early as today. When it comes to discipline, managing your time wisely is one of the must-have skills that you have to have. Especially when you don't want to waste it.

If you are one of the many people who procrastinate and actually want to conquer it, then this is the chapter you don't want to skip. Let's do it now:

IT'S POSSIBLE THAT IT'S THE DUNNING-KRUGER EFFECT OR PERHAPS YOU'RE JUST BEING LAZY

What exactly is the Dunning-Kruger effect? To simply put it into easy to understand terms, it's when people who are deemed incompetent cannot recognize just how incompetent they are. The explanation can go on for a long time, but let's just say that what it boils down to is that people tend to overestimate themselves when it comes to their abilities. You could absolutely suck at something but declare yourself the best in the world (though your actions prove otherwise).

One of the key things that could be the cause of this effect is ego. Are critical tasks that need to be done too good for you? Do you think that you can't be bothered for doing such things that have to be done? The Dunning-Kruger Effect could play a role in procrastinating.

When they say, "I'll do it tomorrow", it's a veiled way of saying "I've got better things to do than that". They are well aware that a certain task is important. But the problem is they refuse to acknowledge the importance at all. The Dunning-Kruger Effect and procrastination do go hand and hand to an extent. Procrastinating on purpose is a prime example.

Laziness and procrastination are not the same thing. But they are similar for one reason: all it takes is a lack of motivation. The major distinction between someone who is lazy and someone who procrastinates is the latter has aspirations (which eventually don't get fulfilled). Laziness is inaction where there are no aspirations to speak of.

PRACTICING DELAYED GRATIFICATION IS DIFFICULT, BUT IT'S DEFINITELY WORTH IT

Delayed gratification is the act of waiting to get what you want. For as long as you have lived, you have already experienced it to some degree. One example is Christmas. The presents sitting under the tree cannot be opened until Christmas morning. You're excited to know what you're getting, but you want to open up your gift now rather than wait later.

Practicing delayed gratification may be hard to do. And it may be a true test of willpower. But the reward at the end when you finally open that Christmas gift is all the more satisfying. Most things are usually worth the wait. Practicing delayed gratification will improve your self-control by leaps and bounds. At the same time, it will also help you achieve your long-term goals much easier and at a quicker rate of speed (without rushing into things, mind you).

Remember that Marshmallow Test we talked about earlier in our chapter about willpower? This is a prime example of delayed gratification at work. It's better to wait for the reward (no matter how sweet and satisfying it is). Though the good feeling of enjoying something may be tempting enough for you to act quickly, it all comes down to disciplining and restraining yourself.

Good things do indeed come to those who wait. But at the same time, those good things will also go to those with the self-control and patience to work hard and keep their eye on the prize. If you practice this, time won't be so much of the evil villain some people make it out to be.

THE POWER TO OVERCOME COMPULSIONS AND TURN AWAY WHEN FACED WITH TEMPTATIONS

Compulsion and temptation is a two-headed monster that many will encounter, but only few will slay. Are you one of the few to do that? First and foremost, let's define both compulsion and temptation. A compulsion is the irresistible urge to act a certain way while temptation is the desire to do something, even if it's not the smartest thing to do. When the two are put together, then that's when the real disaster begins.

Compulsive activities such as gambling, shopping online, or the like may be an unwise thing to do even if you do too much of it. If a compulsive gambler is not playing his or her favorite games online or at a casino, they will feel uncomfortable. But they won't undergo any severe physical withdrawals or anything. However, a compulsive gambler will find themselves in a monetary situation that will be hard to get out of.

Acting on your compulsions will certainly lead you on the road to poor health or financial stability. That's because you have no control over it whatsoever. When there's a cue, there's a signal for you to "go". With temptation, you are aware that the opportunity to gamble or eat when stressed is there. But you are also aware that there's a choice between doing it or not doing it. Those who are compulsive in their actions don't even take one nanosecond to think about it. That's the major difference.

Keep in mind that when you are apart from the things you do on a compulsive level; it's not going to make you sick. No one has even died from being deprived of the compulsive habits that they have done. But those same compulsive habits can lead to poor health problems where your lifespan could be cut short. We're not trying to scare you, but sometimes the truth about such bad habits and behaviors can be hard-hitting.

How exactly can you place a firm grasp on compulsions and temptations. We'll show you how to avoid them before things really get out of control. Here's what they are:

1. Recognize your compulsive behaviors

The first thing to do is recognize what your compulsive behavior is. It's also a good idea to know why you act on this without even thinking. This will challenge you to identify the cues and triggers. You will find out exactly why you act on your compulsions. For example, compulsive gambling could be stemmed by the idea of placing a large risky bet with the chance of winning big. The desire to "get rich quick" and make your existing financial issues go away can drive that compulsive behavior. Think of the feelings and the desires that trigger these behaviors.

2. Be aware of situational selection

Situational selection is something we face every day. Especially in situations where we are hungry or thirsty. Either way, you are faced with plenty of options. Do you go for Burger King or Subway? Coke or water? Get the idea. At this point, you are aware of what you can choose to satisfy your hunger or thirst. However, one option may not be as good as the other. Recognize which option is better for you in terms of the short-term and long-term benefits.

3. Practice situation isolation

Let's say you're in a situation where the temptations will be quite high. If you can't get out of the situation, the best thing you can do is isolate the "temptation". For example, if you are at a party where they serve alcohol and you drink regularly (but play the role of designated driver), stay as far away from the bar as possible. Opt for options that are farther away from your temptations. While it may be hard to do, acting on the opposite of the usual is a lot more rewarding.

4. Know the difference between fun and compulsion

It's one thing to gamble for the fun of it. It's another to do it compulsively. The main difference is self-control. Too much of what seems to be a good thing will always be bad. There is no other way to say it. It's important to distance the fun things from the stressful situations and the like. People use compulsive behaviors to escape from stressful situations or life in general.

5. Find a way to distract yourself from a temptation

We know that we've come down hard on distractions in this book. However, there are times when distracting yourself from something can be a good thing. In this instance, we're talking about pulling yourself away from a temptation. In other words, find something that will reroute your focus on that one thing instead of something you are tempted to do. The more you're into this new distraction, the farther you will distance yourself from the temptation.

6. Find like-minded people who have conquered compulsion and temptation

No one knows about conquering compulsion and temptations better than the people who have done it themselves. It's important for you to seek them out and ask for advice. They will be happy to help you find your way to beating compulsions and temptations. They've been there and done that. The last thing they could ever do is refuse helping those who are going through the same issues they have had in the past.

7. Don't fight, evade

Whoever said that the best way to win a fight is to never get into one obviously got it right. This is true in the case of compulsions and temptations. You'll want to avoid the fight and de-escalate it as much as possible. It doesn't hurt your ego in any way. Fighting your compulsion and temptations will be a waste of time. But you can find a way to isolate yourself from them as far away as possible.

BREAKING THE CYCLE BY TURNING THE NEGATIVE INTO A POSITIVE

Now, you're going to learn how to turn your negative thinking into positive thinking. We have reached the point where negative thinking is pretty much a pointless task to someone who is more disciplined and mentally tough. Having the ability to think positively will help you instill a new set of beliefs. If you repeatedly say good, positive things about yourself then chances are you will absorb those positive beliefs. And it will show.

With that said, let's take a look at some tips on how you can be more positive instead of being negative:

Never play the victim and assume responsibility: These days, it's easy for us to play the victim rather than claim responsibility for our own actions. It's up to you to create your own life. Don't wait for a specific circumstance. You have the option to take action or sit on the sidelines.

Say more positive than negative: It's true that if you say things that are negative or positive, you become that. Say it again and again and it will be embedded in your brain. If you have a can-do attitude and speak the same language, you will slowly adopt a can-do mindset.

Accept that no one is perfect (and neither are you): Anyone who says they are "perfect" in every way is a liar. No one is. And neither are you. When you expect to be perfect but fall short of your own expectations, that will discourage you from being positive. Doing the best, you can is a lot better than doing nothing at all.

Assess what you are thankful for: Take a moment and write down five things that you are thankful for. Focusing on this will help instill positive thoughts in your mind rather than the negative ones.

Be able to catch yourself: Some people think negatively and will let it flow through them. However, if you are making the switch between negative and positive, catch yourself thinking or saying those things. For example, instead of saying "I suck" you can say "I'm not that good, but I know I can improve". Sound simple enough, right?

YOUR TIME IS PRECIOUS, DON'T WASTE IT

Without question, time is a valuable asset in our lives. We can invest in it wisely or waste it. When you lose time, it's gone for good. You can never recover it. But when it's used to your advantage, the return on investment will be even greater. With that said, saying that "you don't have the time" is not a valid excuse. That's just a veiled way of saying "I don't have my priorities in order".

Keep in mind that there are 24 hours in a single day. Everyone is allocated the same amount of time in a day. It's how you spend it that matters most. Or better yet, it's a matter of how you prioritize your time. You should invest your time in things that you consider a high priority. The truth is, time can be taken away from anyone at any given time. The average person lives to be roughly 74 years old. People can live longer or shorter than that. That's why you should never underestimate time in the slightest.

That's why it is important to say "no" to the things that are a waste of time. It's better to invest time in getting the critical tasks done. When you do, you get a vast return on investment that can be spent on whatever you want (such as spending time doing the things you enjoy the most).

Unless someone invents a time machine or turns a DeLorean into one, we will never be able to turn back time. Spend it wisely or don't, the choice is yours.

TIME MANAGEMENT STRATEGIES THAT WILL CHANGE THE WAY YOU LIVE YOUR LIFE

Now, we'll be taking a look at some of the time management strategies that have long been tested and proven to work. Managing your time wisely will be key when it comes to instilling self-discipline in yourself. By the time you learn these strategies, some of these will stick out in more ways than one. You can even use one of these to help you invest more of your time in the important things rather than something that will give you a negative return.

Here are the time management strategies that you want to try out for yourself:

1. Plan and prioritize

As mentioned earlier, the excuse of "not having the time" is translated as "not having your priorities in order". You want to put the most critical tasks of your day up front every day before working on other tasks. That way, you invest in the true priorities that matter most. This can take some time. Especially when you are learning to recognize the real priorities from the ones that don't need a lot of focus at the moment.

2. Begin the day with a clear focus

When you get up in the morning, the last thing you want to wake up to is having your mind racing with seven billion different things. You want to wake up with a clear focus on what needs to be done today. You've already planned it the night before. Now, it's time to act on it. Focus on one thing and then switch to another when the task is done.

3. Eliminate procrastination

Obviously, procrastination is the enemy of time management. If you are going to say you're going to do something, you do it. Be someone whose words are like iron. Make it firm by doing what you say you are going to do. To say that you're going to do something, but never doing it will make you look bad. The sooner you get it done, the better.

4. Don't worry about multi-tasking

Multi-tasking can actually do more harm than good (contrary to what everyone else is saying). Simply put, focusing on one thing at a time and investing your time in that will definitely put you a head above shoulders over those who claim to be the world's greatest multi-tasker.

5. Recognize and minimize potential interruptions

If you are aware of some of the interruptions that may throw you off your game, identify them. Next, you want to distance yourself from them as much as possible. If checking your email or social media while in the middle of something is what you do, try to stop doing it and wait before you are finished with the task you're working on.

6. Split up larger projects

If you have a large project that can't get done in a day, it's better to break them up into small pieces. They can be split up into the tiniest of fractions. Day by day, hour by hour, and so on. The last thing you want to do is take on a gargantuan task and take as little breaks from it as possible.

7. Delegate any tasks that you can't work on

Is there something you can't focus on? Is there something that you can't do because you don't know how? The answer is simple: delegate. When you delegate tasks, it will alleviate any pressure you may have on yourself. Give the task to someone who is knowledgeable enough to get it done.

8. Rest and recharge

Resting up and recharging your batteries to do it all over again is essential. Without a good night's rest, you won't be able to focus on the tasks at hand the next day. Don't take all night and sacrifice sleep because something has to be done. Everyone has their limits...even you.

RECAP

Time management is easy to do now that you know how to get it done. Procrastination can exist in the form of the Dunning-Kruger effect or a lack of capitalizing on your aspirations. Procrastination should not be considered a form of laziness since those who are lazy lack aspirations. When reaching your goals or completing the tasks that will reward you, you'll feel a sense of satisfaction like no other. But when the timing is longer than usual, that can trigger delayed gratification. You know that the rewards are satisfying, but you will wait a long enough time to earn it. Delayed gratification is a true test of discipline and willpower that you can pass with flying colors (you've already done it as a kid just days before Christmas, mind you).

Overcoming compulsions and temptations will require you to isolate yourself from them as opposed to fighting them. Identify the reasons why your compulsive habits exist and find a way to lessen its power, so you are not so easily pulled in.

It's also important to switch your negative thinking into positive. When you think positive, it will show in your mindset, your body language, your words, and so on. And remember that time is a precious thing that you cannot lose. Once you waste a second, you never will get it back.

Lastly, managing your time will yield tremendous results when done right. When investing in your time wisely, your return will be far greater. And it can be spent on the things you enjoy most.

12

IT'S WITHIN YOUR GRASP,
LITERALLY

Being able to have discipline and mental toughness within your reach is something you want to acquire. For most, it's farther away from them with every passing day. At this point, discipline and mental toughness are literally right in front of you. It's like an opportunity that is waiting to be taken by the right person. And people will tend to walk past it like they never notice it.

In this chapter, we're going to talk about the endowed progress effect. We'll explain what it is and how it pertains to discipline and mental toughness. When you are rewarded for your efforts and hard work, it's a good feeling knowing that you've started from point A and finished at point B. But what if you got something more than that? How would you feel if the reward was even greater than expected? Let's talk about that right now.

TRICK YOUR BRAIN USING THE ENDOWED PROGRESS EFFECT

The endowed progress effect is simply defined as receiving a bonus on top of your original reward for a job well done. For example, let's say you have a sales job and your goal is to sell at a rate of 20 percent. You successfully double the percentage and have a 40 percent sales rate. Not only are you rewarded for your normal payment, but you also receive a bonus for exceeding your goal.

Another example of endowed progress is a rewards program. Let's say your local coffee shop has a thing where you buy five coffees and get the sixth one free. Your loyalty to the business and buying the same item over and over again can give you a reward. It instills the reward that comes with the habit of coming into the coffee shop frequently.

When tricking your brain with the endowed progress effect, you are looking to work hard at achieving your goal and earning a much greater reward for completing it. That extra "reward" will motivate them to get the job done even though they actually won't earn something on top of the original reward in the end. Also, the endowed progress effects gets people to think that they have a head start towards completing the tasks at hand.

With that said, it's important to get a head start on achieving the goal. On top of that, using abstract measurements to track your progress will help you stay the course and complete the goal you are focusing on. Also, you want to focus on the time you already spent as opposed to the time you're about to invest in. That will give you the mentality of "I put this much time in it, I might as well continue". Also, focus on what's left to do as opposed to what's already done. Transparency is key when it comes to getting the job done.

PRACTICE DISCIPLINE AND PRODUCTIVITY USING BULLET JOURNALING

If there is one thing that you should consider doing while on the path of becoming more disciplined and productive it is using a bullet journal. What exactly is a bullet journal? A bullet journal is used to track everything in your life both in the personal and business side of it. You can write down something like a "to-do list" or a list of weekly plans that you can write out and execute. You can also use it to track things like income and expenses throughout the week. It's a to-do list, financial planner, and corkboard all rolled into one. And putting one to good use can help you become more disciplined and more productive in your tasks. So long as you consult and update it on a regular basis, it will definitely help you out in the long run.

You don't have to make it a very creative bullet journal. It can be organized and to the point. That way, you'll find your to-do list for the week or find an item on the list that you can get done in the next day rather than two days out. Bullet journals are fun to keep up on once you are able to get the hang of them.

BE SMART IN USING YOUR SMARTPHONE

Sure, we've been hard on the smartphone throughout a good part of this book. But we don't want you to give up on it entirely. There are ways to rely on it. Especially in a way that will help you keep track of your progress and remind you to perform certain tasks. A smartphone can be useful in terms of education. Most people will reach for their smartphones to access something educational versus their desktop computer.

Not only that, but you can also use a wide variety of apps designed for many things like task management, keeping track of your daily and weekly activities and so on.

The advantages and disadvantages of using a smartphone

What exactly are the advantages and disadvantages of using your smartphone? While there are some good things about using your smartphone, we cannot forget about the not so good things about them. Sometimes they are useful and sometimes they can be a distraction. Let's look closely at each advantage and disadvantage:

Advantages

- You can keep in touch with friends and family via text, phone call, and social media
- Play games, music, and movies anywhere you go
- Be able to set reminders to perform various tasks using specific apps that you can download on your phone
- You have it on you in the event of an emergency
- You can check your bank balance to see if you have any money on you at any given time thanks to apps provided by your bank.

Disadvantages

- Can be a distraction during times where focus on a priority task is needed
- Increased use has been linked to loneliness and other mental health issues
- Can cause sleep deprivation due to the blue light emitting from the screen
- May cause a lack of awareness around you (especially in a dangerous situation).

While using your smartphone can work to your advantage, there may be times where using it may not be necessary. You can use it to help you form good habits (if it's used properly). It's all about self-control and being able to know your boundaries. You can use it in your free time once you have completed the tasks and priorities you have planned for the day.

ATTAIN EFFICIENCY WITH MORE RELIABLE APPS AND TOOLS

Now, we'll be talking about some of the best apps and tools that we believe are essential in keeping track of your activities while building discipline and good habits. These are apps you can download and access on your smartphone. Some of them can also be accessed on your desktop or laptop computer. Either way, you'll be within reach of most of these apps.

You can use these apps on a regular basis so you can stay focused and keep track on what you've accomplished and what is left to do. We'll also explain why these apps may be beneficial to you as well. Let's start with the first app on the list:

1. Todoist

If you are looking for the best app to help keep a to-do list well organized, look no further than Todoist. Whether you sign up via email or by using your Facebook or Google account, you'll have to set up your to-do list that you can get done throughout the day or week. You can add new tasks or cross them off the list just by a couple touches of your finger or by using the sound of your voice. Either way, it makes to-do lists very efficient.

The best thing about this app is that it tracks your "Karma points". For every task that you get done on time, you earn more points. For every task that is overdue or finished beyond the due date, your "karma" will take a hit. It's the perfect rewards system to have in place for a to-do list app.

2. SimpleNote

Do you like taking notes? Do you have an idea so awesome that you have to write it down before you forget? Either way, SimpleNote will help you keep everything tidy in one handy little app. If you hate note taking apps that are loaded with so many features, this app will be something you might enjoy. After all, you don't want an app that will be hard to navigate and has plenty of clutter.

Best of all, it's free to use and is compatible with Android and iOS

3. Habitica

If you enjoy playing RPG-like games, then we've got some good news for you. Habitica is the best habit building app that will give you game-like features that will help you build more good habits with ease. Want to quit a bad habit and switch to a good one? Set it and level up with each small task you accomplish. Like Todoist, it has a reward system that will work to your advantage every time you accomplish something by the deadline. It can also "punish" you for tasks that are overdue or completed late.

Another great thing we like is the community feature. You can connect with like-minded people who are trying to form good habits and cheer them on as they are en route to building better habits. There is no better way to form better habits faster than having a solid support system.

4. Google Tasks

If you are a fan of Google's myriad of apps, thankfully there's a task app just for you. One of the cool things about this app is that it does the prioritizing for you. If you have critical tasks that you need to accomplish first thing, the app will help organize it to where tasks with the highest priority are on the top of the list.

This will also sync with your Gmail account and will also be accessible across other devices. If your Google account is linked to your devices, you'll have access to your task list. Your Google Calendar will be automatically filled with these tasks on your to-do list. That way, you are pretty much reminded to get it done everywhere you go.

5. Zoom

This app has gained a lot of fame in the past year. Especially when COVID-19 had most people scrambling to find alternative ways to meet up without the in-person contact. Zoom is perfect whenever you are running a business, conversing with family, or when you are taking a class.

With high-quality audio and video calls, keeping in contact with the people who matter most is easier than ever. Will we see the rise of Zoom meetings as opposed to in-person meetings going forward? That's a possibility. Especially when it will also reduce commute times for most people.

6. Asana

We've already looked at apps that focus on individual tasks. But what about for small groups and teams? Leave that all to Asana. This will allow you to set up tasks for your team members and help them keep track of their progress. You'll be able to set and assign tasks, prioritize them by setting deadlines, and set specific details so everyone on the team follows along and does what is assigned to them. If you are looking for the perfect app that is easily accessible and great for keeping track of everyone's progress, Asana is the go-to app.

7. Cold Turkey Blocker

If you are looking for something that will reduce distractions while working on your computer, Cold Turkey Blocker will come in handy. All you have to do is program it to where it will "block" websites that will serve as your distractions (i.e. -- Facebook, Twitter, etc.). When this is activated, try and access Facebook or any website you choose to block. You won't get through it. All you need to do is switch it on or schedule the app on when to block the websites in question and you'll be in business.

RECAP

Discipline and mental toughness may be within reach even when you are working on bettering yourself. At the same time, you can keep track of your progress while using your smartphone. Your smartphone is not your enemy when you are using it for all the right things. There are advantages to using them, but keep in mind that there are disadvantages that may hinder your level of discipline and mental toughness.

Be sure to check out the many apps that will help you manage your time, keep organized, and stay on task throughout the day. The seven listed above are just a sample of the dozens of apps that are available to download on both your smartphone and your computer.

V

APPLYING DISCIPLINE AND MENTAL TOUGHNESS IN YOUR LIFE

13

YOU MUST UNSTUCK YOURSELF

One of the things that people say is "I'm stuck". Especially when they are trying to make a move from one point to the next. This chapter will show you how to make yourself "unstuck". We have reached the point that getting "stuck" is just an excuse for saying you don't want to get something done. Or perhaps you are waiting for something or someone to motivate you.

The truth is that those who stay stuck will never get anything done. We have a section dedicated to that and we'll dive into it shortly. As mentioned earlier in the book, when you intend to find motivation, it's mostly elusive. It's like a cat or a dog. It will come to you if it feels comfortable enough to approach you. As weird as it sounds, what we're trying to say is the last thing you want to do is "chase" motivation.

When getting the job done, you will know that motivation has arrived. There will be no stopping you when you start. If you are looking for a new way to obtain the motivation without even thinking about it, keep reading. This chapter will hand you the new way to get motivated (even if you've failed to find it in the past). Let's get going:

YOU DON'T FEEL LIKE DOING IT? THEN YOU'LL NEVER END UP DOING IT

Earlier on, we have said that the more you keep saying negative things, the more you will become it. This is such a case when you say, "I don't feel like doing this or that". For this reason, when you repeat this process, you develop this habit of not wanting to get anything done. So, you end up not doing it. This is one of the symptoms of procrastination or laziness (depending on whether or not you have the aspirations to do something).

People are looking for those "perfect moments" to get started on some task. Otherwise, what's the point in getting it done? Here's the thing: if you are looking for a "perfect moment", we can finally unveil it right here to the world. We're so excited we can't wait any longer. The perfect time to get started on something is...drum roll please...right now! Yes, there is no "perfect moment" better than right now to get something done.

Waiting for the perfect moment is a complete waste of time. And remember, the time you waste is the time you never get back. It's as simple as that. You can accept this fact and get started or you can be a prime example of the Dunning-Kruger Effect and be aware of that while choosing not to take action. Either way, the choice is yours.

Remember this age-old quote: "The best time to grow a tree was 20 years ago. The second-best time is now".

JUST GET THE BALL ROLLING

At risk of turning this into a physics textbook, we quote the following from Newton's First Law of Physics: "Objects at rest tend to stay at rest. Objects in motion tend to stay in motion". Obviously, the point is you need to get moving in order to get something done. There are some things that will obviously help you get the ball rolling. Clearly, motivation itself is not one of them. You need to find a starting point to ensure that you build up as much momentum as possible so you can move on from one task to the next with little to no issue.

Getting started on something can be as simple as visualizing the action itself and the outcome that follows. Think of the reward that you'll earn for a job well done. Also, think about what could happen if you don't get the job done? Visualizing it and incorporating the emotion within it may be enough to get the ball rolling.

Another thing is to program your mind into being in the moment. You can do that by focusing on the breathing techniques that we've discussed in the chapter on mindfulness. To have a clear mind that is laser focused on the now will help you achieve a focus like nothing else. When you are focused, that's when the ball moves. And when it moves, it keeps moving until the task is complete. But if it's a task that requires a lot of time, do part of the work, take a break, and keep going.

There are small tasks that you must complete before getting started. Get one out of the way, on to the next one. And so on. Remember, the small tasks will help you stay focused. And it's one step closer to getting whatever you need to finish said and done with. We guarantee you that you won't be overwhelmed in the slightest.

One thing to remember about motivation. It's not motivation that starts moving the ball. It's what keeps the ball moving. In other words, **motivation is momentum**. As long as you start with the vision of succeeding at your goals in your mind, motivation will find you when you keep going.

MAKE INFURIATING TASKS BEARABLE

In every task we perform or every job we work at, there is always one thing that we absolutely hate to do. For example, if you work at a convenience store, some of your tasks may include changing the inside and outside trash cans. Another task is cleaning the bathrooms. They are dirty jobs, but someone has to do them in order to keep the place clean. You'll notice that a lot of people hate doing the dirty jobs, so they shift the responsibility to someone else. Naturally, it may anger you.

However, it shouldn't anger you. It should give you the opportunity to prove yourself to others that unlike themselves, a task that is unbearable doesn't bother you in the slightest. Your boss may notice that and may praise you for it. The point is that not every person on Earth has the mental strength nor the positive frame of thinking to do the "dirty jobs".

But not every unbearable task has to be dirty. They do however require you to make decisions that could change the entire trajectory of someone's life or career. It could even change the path of an entire business. Sometimes, you will be faced with two decisions that will have negative results at the other end. And it will impact someone or something in a way you don't want to see. So, making a decision where the impact is not as severe is what you're gunning for. It's a decision that you don't want to make, but deep down it's the best course of action going forward.

Unbearable tasks can also be "boring" as well. One way to make them as less boring as possible is to find something interesting about the task. It doesn't matter how ridiculous it sounds. Plus, you don't have to share that observation with other people. Just find something that makes the task less boring to do. You can also use the opportunity of performing a boring task to sharpen your mindfulness. Feel the task, hear the sound of it, and make the smallest observations that no one seems to notice. It's a lot better than doing it on autopilot while grumbling about it, right?

IMAGINE THE FUTURE AHEAD OF YOU

Visualizing the future and what you can accomplish can help you drive yourself to start achieving the tasks at hand. Imagining a future where you are able to accomplish anything with little to no delay may just be enough for you to get the ball rolling. A fulfilling, positive future is what we aim for. We don't want to be stuck with the same old, same old six months or even a year down the road. While the future may be bright for us, you still need to focus on the now in order to see it in full view.

One of the visualization techniques that will work to your advantage when thinking about the future is known as the 10-10-10 rule. The way it works is this: Imagine a decision that you are about to make. It's something that will have some degree of impact over the course of time. What you want to do is visualize the decision as if you made it already. How will it impact you 10 minutes after the fact? How about 10 months? Now try 10 years?

It sounds like there is some kind of ripple effect that occurs with just one decision you've made. It can also have some kind of impact on the rest of the decisions and life events that will occur in the future. Especially the ones that will happen ten minutes from now. This is why visualization is so important. You can think about making the decision and think about how you feel about it.

In 10 months or 10 years' time, you'll feel like you could have done something different. Or you can feel good knowing that it was the right decision and you don't regret making it. Either way, it will have an effect on you long after you've made the decision yourself. Before making a vital decision, use the 10-10-10 rule to your advantage when visualizing what will likely happen once it's made.

The lesson here is that every decision will have short-term and long-term effects. Whether they will be negative or positive will depend on what you've decided on. If anything, this will give you a chance to ponder your decisions and choose the right one without hesitation.

PUSHING THROUGH, EVEN ON THE WORST DAYS

In life, there will be good days and bad days. And there will be the worst days of your life. Even on those days, it's better to get through them the best that you can. One of the caveats of pushing through on your worst days is that you still need to keep your limits in the front of your mind. You don't want to push yourself too far or it will have adverse effects on your health (both mentally and physically).

Working through your worst days will be one of the ultimate tests of your discipline and mental toughness. You will have negative emotions running through your mind. It's okay to be sad or angry about things. And remember, being mentally tough does not mean becoming an emotionless robot. However, you don't want your emotions to overcome you to the point where the decisions you make will be solely based on your emotions without a hint of logic. It will likely throw things off course.

Even on your worst days, the key here is to find the good among the bad. For example, what would happen if you just took a deep breath, took it slow, and gave yourself enough time to gather your thoughts and make an important decision that could affect your future? Things may turn out for the better because you gave it some thought rather than let your emotion cloud your judgement.

It's okay to make mistakes. It's okay to keep going when the day isn't going your way. All that matters is that the emotions of it all should not get to you. One thing that will make you feel better through all the bad stuff happening in one day is the positive feelings you'll get whenever you complete the tasks that need to be finished. You will feel a lot better in ten minutes after finishing it. Not to mention, you will feel good about it 10 months and 10 years afterwards. You will think back on that day and remember some of the positives that happened instead of the bad.

DOPAMINE CAN BE YOUR BEST FRIEND OR WORST ENEMY

Dopamine is the chemical in your brain that makes you feel good about things. It can be your best friend or your worst enemy depending on the situation (or the decisions you make). Either way, you need to frame your mind as to how dopamine can serve you best. When you are eating something unhealthy, dopamine is released to make you feel good about eating something tasty. But the reality is, dopamine in this situation is like that friend who will say things about loyalty and respect but turn around and stab you in the back years later. In this context, when eating junk food, you will suffer the long-term consequences such as weight gain and the potential health effects that go along with it.

You can also get a dopamine rush by doing something that will have a positive effect on you in the long run (especially for your health). It's about training your mind to release that dopamine whenever you do the right things. So how do you go about doing this? You could do what is known as a "dopamine fast". This could mean avoiding the usual activities that you do in order to make you feel good about it. This might mean eliminating smartphone use for a short period of time. Or it could mean not talking to people for a set time period (which may be risky for those who tend to be more social). It's about finding that one task that releases a good amount of dopamine and cutting that out of your life temporarily to reset your brain.

The jury is still out on whether or not it works. But you could try it for a short period like a week. After that period, you can decide to do it for another week. Do it until you feel that there is a shift in your brain where you can get the dopamine rush you need from the things you can get done as opposed to the things that make you lazy or inactive.

Even if you finish a task where you had a hard time getting started, the feeling of getting it done anyway will guarantee that dopamine rush. And it will be the first of many if you keep doing it.

RECAP

If you are stuck, the best way to get unstuck is to get moving anyways. There is no point in waiting for the right moment or searching for that motivation. You visualize the future of performing the task and what happens after that. Remember, every decision you make will have an impact on you ten minutes, ten months, and ten years from now. In those future time frames, will you feel good about it? Or will you wish that you took the action when the opportunity presented itself?

You will also be faced with tasks that no one will like to do. It's up to you to set the example that even though the task is not something you enjoy; someone has to do it anyway.

Visualizing the future will be key in accomplishing something. Especially if you are having the worst day of your life. There will be worse days. And it will be up to you to put your discipline and mental toughness to the test in order to get through them. You will feel good and have that moment of positivity once you get something done.

That rush of dopamine will certainly make you feel like the tasks you're supposed to do are effortless. However, the dopamine release can seduce you into making bad decisions only if you allow them to happen.

KEEPING YOURSELF FIT AND HEALTHY

W hile discipline and mental toughness will spread out through all aspects of your life, you should also remember to utilize it when you want to live a healthy and fit lifestyle. Sure, the road to living a life where you are healthier and in better shape will be a bumpy one. Yet, at this point you should have the awareness and knowledge that you will need to incorporate discipline and mental toughness to start the journey, continue on it, and get to the destination.

Every person has unique goals when it comes to living a healthy life. Some may want to lose 20 pounds while some will want to lose just 10 pounds. Either way, there is a goal out there that you can set and achieve. Plus, it will be a lot easier to get there as long as you are aware of any potential setbacks that may pop up out of nowhere.

We'll talk about discipline and how it should be as routine as brushing your teeth. We'll also discuss which exercise routine will work to your advantage. We'll also talk about other habits that will tie into being healthy and fit such as your diet and getting a good night's rest. While we are not fitness experts in the slightest, this chapter will save you a lot of time and will help give you a better understanding of how living a fit and healthy life ties in with discipline and mental toughness.

Keep reading if you are looking to make amends on your life when it comes to your overall fitness:

DISCIPLINE WILL MAKE MASTERING THE FUNDAMENTALS OF HEALTH AND HAPPINESS AS ROUTINE AS BRUSHING YOUR TEETH

The truth is, discipline will be one of the key building blocks in making sure that you stay on top of your health and fitness. It is important to instill self-discipline since it will help you make decisions with a better understanding of the consequences or results (depending on the magnitude of them). By this we mean the following: if you were hungry and had to choose between McDonalds and Subway, which one would you go with? On paper, the choice is obvious. Subway has much healthier options compared to McDonalds (despite the fact that the latter serves up salads as their only healthy option).

If you eat junk (albeit on a consistent basis), that will negatively affect your overall health and fitness. However, if you choose to restrain yourself from eating it and opt for something healthier instead, that's a good sign. Self-discipline is the ability to restrain yourself and give into the temptation of something that may taste good, but can really hurt you in the long run.

With discipline, you can easily say "no" to the junk food and yes to the foods that will help you build muscle, perform better in the gym, and ward off any ailments that can get serious in a moment's notice. Also, self-discipline will keep you on the right path in terms of how you use alcohol. Instead of binge drinking or getting drunk, you can use moderation. Self-discipline can also help you stay away from drugs, which some people will use to "escape" life in general.

With consistent self-discipline, you are less likely to make impulsive decisions. You will be able to think clearly and use your head when making a decision. Of course, impulsive decisions don't require you to think about your choices and actions. The deeper you embed discipline into your mind, the more routine it will become.

Discipline will help you set forth a routine that will ensure that you stay in shape for as long as possible. Imagine getting up in the morning and ready to do a quick one-mile jog before the day begins. Or getting out of bed, doing a couple sets of kettlebell swings and call it done in 10 minutes. With routine discipline, it will be like second nature.

YOUR DAILY EXERCISE ROUTINE

First off, your daily exercise routine can be done at a time of the day where there is a good amount of time to yourself. Usually it's in the early morning hours. For some, it can be later than that. However, the first thing you need to do before setting up an exercise routine is choosing the time block that works best for you. We have 24 hours in a day. There is at least a block of one hour that will be considered "free".

Remember, if you "don't have the time", you want to straighten out your priorities. So, what exactly is your daily exercise routine? Does it have to be at the gym? The good news there is you don't have to go to the gym in order to incorporate a daily exercise routine. It can be as simple as doing it at home using a yoga mat, a kettlebell, or both. You want your exercise routine to be as simple as possible (even if you do have a little bit of time on your hands).

The key here is that you want it not only to be simple, but it also requires small steps. Obviously, with fitness there will be times when you'll be doing the same thing over and over again. Three sets of 12 repetitions of one exercise (and the same for the other exercises you have planned out for the day). The more you keep doing it, the stronger and fitter you become.

SIMPLE EXERCISES TO TRY OUT

If you have never had a fitness routine before and want to start, we'll show you how to put one together with the help of these simple exercises we'll list below. Not only will you be able to choose a couple to start, but you can put one together where you can do a combination of a few exercises per day that focus on specific areas of the body.

Here are some simple exercises that you should consider trying out for yourself (even if you don't have a clue how to set up a fitness routine):

1. Lunges

If you are looking for an exercise that will help with balance and leg strength, lunges are one of the most reliable exercises around. To perform lunges, here's what you'll need to do:

- Stand with your feet at shoulder width and your arms down at the side
- Using your right leg, step forward and bend your knee. Stop when your thigh is parallel to the floor. Also, make sure your foot does not extend past your knee
- With your right foot, push off and return to the standing position. That's one lunge. Now, do the same thing but this time with your left leg.

2. Push ups

One of the most popular forms of calisthenics widely practiced today is push-ups. This will help with building upper body strength. Plus, there are some variations that you can try once you get the hang of them. But for now, let's stick to the basics. To perform push-ups, this is how you do them:

- Start in the plank position. Your body should be upwards with your arms in a straightened position
- Bend your elbows and lower your body down to the floor. Make sure that your chest barely touches the floor or at least an inch off of it. Make sure your elbows are close to your body when doing this

- Return to the plank position. That's one push up. Repeat with as many as necessary. You can start with five, ten, or fifteen. As you get the hang of it, you can try and perform as many until failure.

3. Squats

The good thing about squats is that you can do them with weights or just by using your own bodyweight. For the sake of keeping it basic, this and other exercises will require no weights. With that in mind, let's learn how to squat:

- In a standing position, make sure that your feet are a shoulder's width apart
- Take your arms and raise them behind your head. You can clasp your hands behind your head or raise your arms straight ahead at chest level
- Brace your core and keep your head and chest straight. Then lower your hips and bend your knees. The motion will be as if you are sitting down. Hold the down position for one second and return to the standing position. That's one squat
- Do as many squats as necessary or have a set number in place.

4. Burpees

Now, this is where things will get really challenging. And if you love challenges (you probably do at this point), you might want to give burpees a try. These may be the closest you can get to a full body workout (with a little bit of cardio involved). How do you pull off a burpee? Let's show you how:

- Start in the standing position with your feet at shoulder width
- Bend your knees as if you are doing a squat. Once you reach the low point, transition into the plank position and do a push up
- After performing the push up, return to the up position and jump up in the air. That is one rep
- If you are a complete newbie, perform three sets of 10 burpees. Make adjustments once you get the hang of it and want more of a challenge.

5. Planks

This may be one of the most challenging ab exercises there is, despite looking so simple to do. To pull off a plank, here's what you need to do:

- Get in position as if you are doing a push up. Or you can rest your arms on the floor while they are in a 90-degree position
- Hold the position and tighten your abdominal muscles. Hold for 30 to 60 seconds.

These five exercises are just a sample of some of the most basic exercises that you can do on a daily basis. You don't have to lift heavy weights to start off with building a reliable fitness routine that can be done almost every day. Also, it would be wise for you to choose a day to rest so your muscles can recover and recuperate.

YOU ARE WHAT YOU EAT

It's true what they say, you are what you eat. In this context, either you are healthy or unhealthy. So, what can you do to assume a healthy identity? Aside from regular exercise, having a healthy diet will be key to living a healthier and fit life. It's even more important to know some of the awesome benefits that eating healthy can provide.

All the essential vitamins and minerals, out there are linked to various health benefits such as strong bones, boosted testosterone levels, clearer skin, and many others. So, it's important to know what you're eating if you are shooting for specific benefits like reducing your risk of heart disease or cancers (especially if it runs in your family).

With the right amount of whole grains, fruits, and vegetables (among others) as part of your diet, you'll be eating a lot healthier than most people. If you are planning on eating healthy, consider adding some fresh fruits and vegetables from the produce section to your shopping list next time. Also, opt for whole grain bread instead of white. Also, you should consider choosing fat-free or reduced fat options for most foods.

IMPROVING YOUR OVERALL HEALTH

Believe it or not, self-discipline is a lifesaver. It will improve your overall health in both the physical and mental sense. If you are not at a level that you are satisfied with, it's important to consider making improvements now rather than later. The first thing you should always do is consult with a doctor. You can start by scheduling a checkup (which should be done every year). Your doctor will be able to assess your health and help you get on the path to a healthy lifestyle. If there are some health issues that are discovered, your doctor may recommend medications or other alternatives to treat it.

If you are dealing with health issues that are mental, there is no shame in seeking help from a professional in the mental health field. It can be a therapist or a psychiatrist. This way, you can talk to someone about your problems. Do not worry, everything is kept with strict confidentiality. But keep in mind that it is okay to talk to someone who you trust whenever you are dealing with mental health issues. Also, keep in mind that you can still acquire mental toughness and discipline even if things aren't going right mentally to begin with.

HOW MUCH SLEEP WILL AFFECT YOUR WHOLE DAY?

They say that you need 7 to 9 hours of sleep per night in order to fully function. The truth is a good night's rest will be beneficial in the way you focus. Not to mention, it's healthy for you to get a good night's rest. When you get the proper amount of sleep, you will wake up refreshed and with an easier ability to focus and use that energy to get the day's work done.

But getting a good night's sleep isn't just for focus. It will also help when you want to improve your physical fitness altogether. When sleeping, your muscles will repair faster and will aid in strengthening them. Plus, those who get a consistent amount of sleep on a nightly basis will be less likely to consume more calories throughout the day. So, it will make weight loss a lot easier for most. Those who sleep poorly will tend to eat more throughout the day.

RECAP

Discipline is one of the cornerstones towards living a healthy and fit lifestyle (both mentally and physically). Not only should you keep yourself in good physical conditions, you should also adopt a diet that will help complement that healthy lifestyle. Even if you have never done any exercises, you can try out some of the basics listed in the chapter.

You are what you eat in terms of your overall health. So do your best to change that if you are eating foods that are not good for you. It's fine to treat yourself so long as it's in moderation. But eating a healthy diet where you get plenty of vitamins and minerals will yield its rewards for the long-term.

Improving your overall health can start by visiting a doctor and maybe a mental health professional (if you are dealing with mental health issues). These are people who live to help get people on the right course so they can live healthy and more fulfilling lives.

CONCLUSION – THINGS THAT YOU SHOULDN'T FORGET

Before we wrap things up, we're going to go over a few things that you shouldn't forget. First off, let us remind you that this book is not one of those "one and done" books. We encourage you to keep this book on hand so you can use it as a reference guide. Building discipline and mental toughness will take time. And you will need something to fall back on in case you are stuck with something. This book will always have the handy instructions that will get you unstuck.

Your journey towards discipline and mental toughness will be one of the most interesting and challenging things you've done in your lifetime. But rest assured, the rewards at the other end will be even sweeter. You will live a fulfilling life where you can get the tasks done at a moment's notice and say "no" to the things that will distract you.

Now, let's take a look at the four major things you should not forget to do:

ALWAYS DO MAINTENANCE

Maintaining your discipline and mental toughness will always need to be done. Just like building your muscles, you want to maintain them regularly by eating a protein-rich diet and working out regularly. What are some of the best ways to do maintenance? First, you should keep track of everything and look over the data again and again. How often are you meeting your goals? How long is it taking you? Is there any data that will point to you making changes and improvements?

Also, you shouldn't take your support network for granted. You should do your best to keep in touch with them and lean on them in times where you feel unsure or stuck on things. They will give you advice, encouragement, and remind you that no matter what, you have what it takes to get the task done. If there are those in your network that tend to be more negative than positive, then it is your responsibility to find a suitable replacement while eliminating the toxic attitudes within your support group.

Your support network doesn't always have to be your most trusted friends and family. It can be like minded individuals online who share the same goals and aspirations as you do. Either way, you'll always have people to turn to when the going gets tough.

One of the last building blocks to maintaining discipline and mental toughness is being persistent. In other words, you keep going. You keep the momentum going no matter what stands in your way. Imagine being a speeding train with no brakes. There are brick walls in the way. And you are going at such a fast rate of speed that those walls don't stand a chance. You bust through them and keep speeding onward.

YOU'RE NEVER ALONE

Of course, you're not the only one that is traveling on the journey. Without them, you won't have a support network of like-minded individuals to turn to. There are more people than you realize that want to instill self-discipline and mental toughness. The good news is, there will be a handful of people who will achieve success. The not so good news is some of them will do a few more attempts before finally being able to get it done. It doesn't matter how long it takes for someone to develop discipline and mental toughness. As long as you're doing it, you'll be just fine.

However, the thing to know is that it can get lonely up at the top. That's because there are many people who will start trying to attempt an ultimate goal. But few will actually make it. Even though the top has a few people, you'll feel alone and feel like you're the only one who has made it. But don't let that thought incorporate any negative feelings. You can still be able to connect with the like-minded people who made it alongside you.

As mentioned before, your support system will also help you become more disciplined and mentally tough. You will always have people to turn to when you have questions to ask or if you are struggling with something. Remember, there is no shame in asking for help. And you should never be too proud to reach out for help. Just know that your support system will always be there whether you are starting from zero or have already become more disciplined and mentally tough.

REMAIN HUMBLE AND COMPASSIONATE

When people finally achieve some kind of success, it's common to see them change in terms of their behavior. When someone wins the lottery (for example), they could let money easily change them and therefore behave in a way where it could affect personal relationships. In short, people who find success will often let it go to their head. They may start acting superior and think they are better than everyone else. The truth is, they are lacking in discipline and humility. Sure, they may have mental toughness. But that's only a facade that can come crumbling down.

When you reach new heights and success in your life, it's important to remain humble and compassionate. Even if you are disciplined and mentally tough, it's always a good idea to remember those who have helped build you up. You will need to give credit to those who have been able to stick with you from day one and beyond. When you are mentally tough and disciplined, you will still need to show compassion for those who may be struggling to achieve their goals (or with life in general). You don't have to help everyone in distress. But you could do your best to point them in the right direction if asked.

Humility will allow you to never lose sight of what you are thankful for. With discipline and mental toughness, you will likely be more compassionate because you have dealt with your own struggles in the past. And you may be the person that helps that person out. Whether the other person accepts that help from you or not is entirely up to them, so don't force it.

There's a good chance that you come from humble beginnings. And you have a better understanding of what it's like to have nothing. Do your part to listen to those who are struggling and help them solve the problem. You may not need to solve it yourself. But you may know someone who will. Also, it won't kill you to be a part of someone's support network as well.

REWARD YOURSELF

Of course, you deserve to reward yourself for all the hard work you have accomplished. When it comes to building up discipline and mental toughness, it's a good idea to reward yourself after you've reached an important milestone. Even the smallest of steps made deserve a bit of reward. If you want to move onto the next task with little to no effort, it's better to reward yourself so you can continue on.

The bigger the tasks, the sweeter the reward. It's kind of like the old "carrot on a stick" trick. With the carrot dangling in front of you, you can be the rabbit that chases after it. Only after a certain period of time where you have accomplished the tasks that will inch you closer to the goal, will you enjoy that carrot for yourself.

Also, you'll want to remember that there will be times when you miss doing a task by accident. It may happen due to forgetfulness. The important thing to do is not be hard on yourself. It's easy to do that when you make a mistake that's trivial and not so much a big deal. So, if you goof up, just accept it and move along. Just remind yourself that it's okay to make mistakes. True discipline is restraining yourself from being negative both in your thoughts and in what you say to yourself.

RECAP

When it comes to discipline and mental toughness, it is better to build it up and maintain it throughout your entire life. The old "set it and forget it" philosophy won't work as it will develop complacency and wipe out all the progress that you have worked on. It's hard work, but it will be a lot easier to maintain it throughout every day of your life.

Another thing to keep in mind is that you will never be alone on your journey. There will be like-minded individuals who will share the same goals and aspirations as you do. They will face similar challenges. And they will see to it that they will fulfill those goals come hell or high water. These people can also become a support network separate from the one that consists of your close friends and family. You won't feel alone on your journey, even though there may be less people at the top of the mountain.

When you finally achieve this success, the last thing you want to do is let the success go to your head. Considering that you have started from zero and understand the struggles of having a lack of discipline and mental toughness, retain that humility and compassion so you can use it as a way to position yourself as the person who has been there before. Especially when you are helping someone out.

Finally, rewarding yourself is key when you want to keep going with achieving the goals you have set. Reward yourself whether it's the little things or when you've reached an important milestone. It is the rewards that will keep you moving forward. And before you know it, it's mission accomplished.

www.ingramcontent.com/pod-product-compliance
Lightning Source LLC
Chambersburg PA
CBHW030242030426
42336CB00009B/221